Handbook in
Social Philosophy

to p.55 dull, not very useful as a text to be
read or studied directly — best use
passing as a reference Handbook ?

Handbook in Social Philosophy

Robert N. Beck
Clark University

MACMILLAN PUBLISHING CO., INC.
New York
COLLIER MACMILLAN PUBLISHERS
London

Macmillan Publishing Co., Inc.
866 Third Avenue, New York, New York 10022

Collier Macmillan Canada, Ltd.

Library of Congress Cataloging in Publication Data

Beck, Robert Nelson (date)
  Handbook in social philosophy.

  Includes index.
  1. Philosophy.   2. Sociology.   I. Title.
B63.B42   100   78-7701
ISBN 0-02-307820-0

Printing: 1 2 3 4 5 6 7 8   Year: 9 0 1 2 3 4 5

Preface

Two decades ago, Peter Laslett observed in his introduction to a collection of papers on social philosophy that, "for the moment, anyway, political philosophy is dead." [1] Six years later, in the second volume of the same series, he cited some recently published books and noted a changed philosophical situation—although he did not feel able to proclaim the resurrection of the field. Today, however, many observers would say that the resurrection is accomplished, and that social philosophy has once again moved to the forefront of philosophical work. In the flurry of activity marking the contemporary scene, this *Handbook* seeks to make its contribution.

Generally, a handbook serves as a kind of intellectual guide for a field of inquiry. It seeks to lay out the chief alternative positions, to develop their meaning and implications, to show something of their sources, to mark their oppositions—in a word, to provide something of a map of the issues and proposed answers which are significant and influential in that field. A handbook is also largely a descriptive enterprise in which explicit critique is kept at a minimum. This procedure has also been largely followed here. But evaluation of alternatives need not be absent in the study and use of a handbook, for focused descriptions of positions necessarily set them in opposition. The reflective, evaluative act that all authors hope to arouse in their readers is generated by such opposition, and this may be a sounder pedagogy than an

[1] *Philosophy, Politics and Society,* New York, 1956, p. vii.

approach which guides—maybe spoon feeds—the critical effort. This *Handbook* attempts to fulfill such goals for social philosophy.

The nine positions presented in the text have been chosen for their importance to social theory, and the six topics covered in each chapter (justification for which is given in the Introduction) have been selected as key issues around which to provide the expositions. The positions, of course, are philosophical ones, and are so identified throughout the text. But their meaning and implications for political theories such as democracy and socialism —theories which often have more than one philosophical foundation—are kept constantly in mind. The order in which the social philosophies are presented is roughly historical in the sense of being correlated with their appearance in the Western tradition. Many instructors may find this order useful, because later positions are often developed, not always with specific references, to be sure, in interaction with earlier philosophies. The expositions of the philosophies in the text, however, are given with only the most necessary of historical references so that, within the limits of accuracy, each chapter stands relatively by itself. This means that teachers who follow a different order of presentation of materials, say a systematic or dialectical one, are not limited to the sequence of positions followed here. Generally, any order of reading can be pursued. At the same time, it should be noted that thinkers from the past as well as from the contemporary world have been selected as their work has been central in the development of positions in social philosophy and has had a continuing influence. Users of this *Handbook* will thus become acquainted with most of the important theorists in social philosophy as well as with the chief alternative positions.

The treatment of two theories in this text, namely Platonism and fascism, may call for special explanation in this Preface. Brief mention of Plato is made in the exposition of classical realism, which is a major channel through which Platonism has had an influence on social thought. But while Plato has had a dominating impact on other philosophies as well, it is a moot point whether Platonism has produced a tradition in social thought in the way realism or, for example, utilitarianism has. For teachers and readers who feel that Platonism should be treated more distinctly than

merely in relation to classical realism, an appendix has been
provided that presents Plato's views on the six problems covered
in the main chapters of the book.

Fascism presents a somewhat different problem. Although
surely an influential, if short-lived, political theory of the twentieth
century, fascism is for many thinkers hardly to be classified as a
social philosophy at all. Still, it is generally agreed that there are
philosophical elements in fascism. Hence, again for readers and
instructors who feel that fascism must be treated at least briefly
in the study of social philosophy, a short appendix on fascism and
its philosophical roots is given.

In general, this *Handbook* is designed to help the reader
understand the chief philosophical sources of social thought, to
serve as a manual for students in courses on social thought, and to
provide a reference tool for scholars not fully at home in philosophy. Bibliographical essays, glossary, and index are included to
serve these ends. Some of these materials, as well as much in the
essays themselves, were first used in an anthology, *Perspectives in
Social Philosophy*, although they were originally prepared to stand
individually as a guide in social philosophy.

Finally, it should be emphasized that the term "social philosophy," examined and defined briefly in the Introduction, is used
here in a broad sense and thus includes such subfields as political
philosophy, aspects at least of philosophy of law, and what some
thinkers have called social ethics. When used in introductions,
definitions of these inquiries, as well as of philosophy and social
philosophy, serve primarily to mark out a field of inquiry; refined
and specialized definitions come more appropriately at the end of
study. This *Handbook* is offered in the hope that that end is
achieved in an informed and knowledgeable way.

R. N. B.

Contents ═══════

Introduction

SOCIAL PHILOSOPHY

Students of society ask a great variety of questions about social process and its institutions. Among them, however, is a group of questions such as why one should prefer one kind of society to another, at what goals a political organization should aim, how political institutions may be judged in terms of criteria and methods, why one should obey a government, and when, if ever, one should not. However disparate they may seem, these questions illustrate two special though interrelated philosophic attitudes, one evaluative, the other analytic. The first seeks to judge society by reference to norms and values; the second analyzes and appraises arguments offered in support of special institutions and practices.

Social philosophy is the attempt by philosophers to provide guidance and answers in order to resolve these types of problems. So viewed, it is a *philosophic critique of social process with reference to the principles underlying social structure and functions.*[1]

[1] The term social philosophy was used by Thomas Hobbes for a general theory of human society; it also appears in the subtitle of J. S. Mill's *Principles of Political Economy* (1848). Some related expressions are political philosophy and philosophy of right, which are generally used as synonyms for social philosophy though some philosophers do suggest certain distinctions among them. Social ethics is sometimes used to refer to an inquiry into the value problems of social life, though for philosophers who view social philosophy as primarily a normative discipline, the term has little distinctive meaning.

1

As an introductory definition, this statement serves to mark out a field of inquiry, though it is admittedly somewhat vague and in need of refinement.

Philosophy is the key word requiring clarification in this definition. Unfortunately, the meaning of philosophy is difficult to convey in a brief phrase. It is derived from two Greek words, *philia* (love) and *sophia* (wisdom), an etymology that is helpful for an understanding of Greek philosophy, but that is not very useful for identifying all the work of philosophers throughout Western history. Wisdom to the Greek meant the understanding of "first truths" like real, good, just, even truth itself, and the application of these first truths to the problems of life. Many philosophers, however, have denied both of these meanings: they reject the existence of first truths, and they believe philosophy should be wholly "theoretical" rather than concerned with guiding conduct.

Perhaps more helpful than any brief formula would be a statement of the chief activities in which philosophers have been engaged over the centuries. Here some clarification is possible, for these activities can be conveniently arranged under four descriptive headings. First is the *speculative* activity. Surveying the results of the science and arts, sometimes including common sense and theology, philosophers have attempted in this activity to develop a comprehensive vision or picture of the universe. Since this constructive effort often transcends the more special disciplines, it is usually pursued by speculative rather than analytic methods. A second activity is generally named *phenomenological*. Here philosophers seek to provide a complete and unbiased description of basic experiences. Some experiences like guilt, obligation, and fear are so covered by interpretation and prejudice that their real nature can be recovered only by highly disciplined efforts. Phenomenology aims to make this recovery. A third activity is *normative* and evaluative, for philosophers try to act as critics by providing standards against which individual and social conduct may be judged and guided. Fourth, in what may be called the critical or *analytic* activity, philosophers strive to achieve clarity about the meaning of basic concepts like true, false, good, and just, and of logical patterns relating to them, that are central to all intellectual work.

These four activities, then, describe philosophers' work. Unfortunately, however, an ambiguity remains even here. Some philosophers see them as interrelated parts of an inclusive philosophical activity; others take them to be four kinds of philosophy from which the student must choose. These alternatives carry different implications for the meaning of social philosophy.

Before relating this material to the meaning of social philosophy, it may be well to list briefly the major kinds of problems faced by philosophers—however they decide to view the above activities. This can be done conveniently in terms of the major fields of philosophy that include first, *epistemology* or theory of knowledge. Here the philosopher asks such questions as: What is the source of knowledge? What is the criterion or test of knowledge? What is the nature of knowledge? The second field of philosophy is *metaphysics* or theory of reality. Metaphysics has traditionally relied on speculative methods, and analytic philosophers have often rejected it, seeing it as an invalid or improper discipline. The metaphysician's concern, however, is with problems such as the meaning of being, the nature of reality, and the principles for understanding the cosmos. Third is a group of inquiries generally called the *normative sciences*, which deals with such values as the good (ethics), the beautiful (esthetics), and the holy (philosophy of religion). "Science" is used in its etymological sense of "organized body of knowledge" and does not refer to modern experimental or natural science. "Normative" refers to questions of value. Social philosophy is often included here as it deals with certain values that cluster around the ideal of justice. Finally, there is a group of rather specialized fields that seek to relate some particular discipline, like science or education, to a more general philosophical position. In the absence of any commonly accepted name, they may be called the "philosophies of."

These many statements about philosophy must now be related to the definition of social philosophy, which has just been classified as one of the normative sciences. As the philosophic critique of the principles underlying social process, social philosophy seeks to develop the arguments that justify political and social institutions, either as they actually are or as they are imagined. If the emphasis of a philosopher is primarily evaluative, social philosophy becomes for him a branch of theory of value, which is the inquiry into the nature and meaning of our value experiences. Some philosophers would even make social philosophy into a branch of ethics, arguing that, since ethics or moral philosophy deals with the most general considerations of values, social philosophy is a matter of their application to the moral questions raised by the social order. On the other hand, if the philosopher's interest is in methods of inquiry and analysis of concepts, his social philosophy will be neutral toward value and will be directed rather toward clarification of terms and arguments, possibly also factual considerations. More speculative philosophers may try to combine these two interests.

In any case, these approaches are alike in that they attempt to examine critically the justificatory arguments for social institutions. In this sense, social philosophy is concerned with principles "underlying" social process, real or ideal. Justification is, among other things, a recourse to principles that coherently support and clarify the conclusions that have been drawn. As has been indicated, philosophers sometimes seek these principles in their theories of value, sometimes in methods of analytic clarification, and sometimes in both ethics and analysis.

However pursued—and the various perspectives covered in the text will reveal great diversity in views of social philosophy itself as well as in conclusions drawn—theories of justification of social institutions will be found to include a number of essential further considerations. Among them is, first, an attempt to understand the nature of associative life. The aspects of man's nature—needs, modes of dependence and independence—stand in certain relationships to society and its institutions. A basic problem for any social philosophy is found in this correlative existence of man and society. Here also is suggested a second justificatory problem. Associated life reflects, or may reflect, a set of associative values toward which social process is directed. These values need clarification and justification. Third, there is the problem of power and authority of the state. Social process must be viewed with reference to control in terms of means (authority) as well as ends (values). Fourth, social control may be specified further in terms of law and rights. Law, with its supporting institutions, is an agent of social control, but it grants to individuals certain powers and privileges. What is, or what should be, the nature of law and its assignments of rights is a central question for all social philosophies. #5- Fifth is the problem of political obligation. The preceding factors in justificatory arguments—association, values, power, law, and rights—raise questions regarding the obligations of individuals to society and state and of state to individuals. What is the nature of these obligations? Are there limits to them? Are there conditions under which political obligations may or should be broken? Finally, much of social philosophy is directed toward fundamental under- #6- standing of the inclusive ideal for society and its institutions whose traditional name is justice.

This sketch of the basic concerns of the social philosopher may be of further aid to the student in demarcing his field of inquiry. But introductory statements must remain just that; in the study of philosophy it is especially important to proceed quickly to the arguments and conclusions themselves. The question, "What is social philosophy?" is itself a philosophical question; it must be asked again at the end of one's investigations. Then it may be answered with greater comprehension. Meanwhile, the student should plunge into the stream of philosophic controversy to examine alternative positions and the grounds offered to justify them.

Bibliographical Essay

Though it is touched upon in most textbooks, social philosophy has not been treated in book-length introductory works as frequently as other areas of philosophy. Among the available texts, however, are A. R. M. Murray, *An Introduction to Political Philosophy*, New York, 1953; H. R. G. Greaves, *The Foundations of Political Theory*, London, 1958; Whitaker T. Deininger, *Problems in Social and Political Thought*, New York, 1965; S. I. Benn and R. S. Peters, *The Principles of Political Thought: Social Foundations of the Democratic State*, New York, 1965; Charles Vereker, *The Development of Political Theory*, New York, 1965; Joel Feinberg, *Social Philosophy*, Englewood Cliffs, N.J., 1973; Richard

Taylor, *Freedom, Anarchy and the Law: An Introduction to Political Philosophy*, Englewood Cliffs, N.J., 1973; and Norman E. Bowie and Robert L. Simon, *The Individual and the Political Order*, Englewood Cliffs, N.J., 1977. Somewhat more advanced is Leo Strauss, *What Is Political Philosophy? And Other Studies*, Glencoe, Ill., 1959. Valuable introductions are also found in many anthologies; see, for example, Peter Laslett *et al.* (eds.), *Philosophy, Politics and Society*, series I-IV, Oxford, 1956–1972; F. A. Olafson (ed.), *Society, Law, and Morality*, New York, 1961; Alan Gewirth (ed.), *Political Philosophy*, New York, 1965; and R. P. Wolff (ed.), *Political Man and Social Man*, New York, 1966.

Many materials for the study of social philosophy are presented in historically oriented works. The student should familiarize himself with his library's collections in history and political science as well as in philosophy. A great variety of books on individual thinkers and on movements and schools will be found. Among these are the Home University Library series; the series edited by F. J. C. Hearnshaw from 1923 on, which includes volumes from medieval thought through the Victorian age; John Bowle's two volumes, *Western Political Thought*, London, 1947, and *Politics and Opinion in the Nineteenth Century*, Oxford, 1954; W. A. Dunning, *A History of Political Theories*, 3 vols., New York, 1910–1920; vol. 4, C. E. Merriam and H. E. Barnes (eds.), 1924; John Plamenatz, *Man and Society*, 2 vols., New York, 1963; G. H. Sabine, *A History of Political Theory*, New York, 1937, and later editions; and Quentin Skinner, *Foundations of Modern Political Thought*, Cambridge, 1977. William Ebenstein, *Great Political Thinkers*, 3rd ed., New York, 1960, contains a valuable annotated bibliography.

The cutting edge of contemporary work in social philosophy is found in journals. Most philosophy journals contain articles on social issues, and these can be found by consulting the important bibliographical guide, *The Philosopher's Index*. Three journals specializing in social philosophy are *Philosophy and Public Affairs*, *The Journal of Social Philosophy*, and *Social Theory and Practice*.

Classical Realism

Fundamental to the first position we shall study, in fact, almost its defining characteristic, is the attempt to understand man, society, and government against the background of the cosmos. The questions asked and the answers given, however diversely the particular details may be developed by individual thinkers, arise within the context of a broader theory of the nature of things and of the universe as a whole. In a general sense, the social philosophy of classical realism may be called cosmological or metaphysical.

What is classical realism? The word classical is used to indicate that this position (it is one of the oldest and most continuously active philosophies) had its origin in ancient Greece as well as to distinguish it from other forms of realism such as Scottish common sense realism and American new realism. The term realism identifies a philosophy which holds that the universe consists of real, independent, existing things, hierarchically structured and related, and forming a *cosmos* or totality within which a meaningful and ordered life becomes possible for man. To many readers this definition may seem to be only "common sense," and indeed the realist does hold that his philosophy acknowledges and remains true to the beliefs of the "common man." Yet realism is not simply common sense; in its attempt to articulate the meaning of experience, it becomes a technically developed philosophy.

Three fundamental philosophical assertions are made by the

7

#1 - realist.[1] First, he believes that metaphysics, defined as the science of being, is a valid and important discipline and that, in fact, the concern for being and its principles is the central philosophical #2 -interest. Second, the realist holds in his epistemology that beings can be known by the human mind as they are in themselves. Reason is the agent of such knowledge—hence the realist's insistence on rationality—and truth can be grasped by man as universal, #3 absolute, and eternal. Third, the realist asserts that knowledge of being, especially of human being, provides man with reliable norms of good and evil, both for the individual and for society.

In developing these theses, realists rely heavily on the Greek philosophical tradition as expressed by Plato (427–347) [2] and above all by Aristotle (384–322). Even today, although perhaps in a somewhat modified form, this tradition, which articulates a number of assumptions of Greek life, is a major alternative in philosophy. One of these assumptions was suggested above by the use of the word "cosmos." This nearly untranslatable Greek word carried a number of meanings for the educated Greek. As he applied the word to the universe, he meant that reality is an ordered whole, that law and reason are written into the very nature of things, and that the world is ultimately harmonious and structured. This cosmos, in turn, is to a large extent knowable, and the instrument of knowledge is reason. The regularities, laws, and principles of the universe, themselves rational principles, are available to qualified, inquiring minds. Furthermore, it is important for men to know the laws of reality. Human life is often, to be sure, not harmonious or structured; indeed, it often has the opposite characteristics. To become meaningful, to become lawful and good, life and society must be directed and ordered so as to mirror the objective structure of the universe. The microcosm or little world within man must reflect the order of the macrocosm without, and the instrument of this reflection is reason.

[1] See the platform by a contemporary professional organization, the Association for Realistic Philosophy, in *The Return to Reason*, ed. John Wild, Chicago: Henry Regnery Co., 1953, pp. 357–63.

[2] See Appendix I for an exposition of Plato's views and his position on the six problems covered in this chapter.

Early and medieval Christianity, whose philosophical expression is also included within classical realism, modified these Greek assumptions in the light of revelation and belief in a personal, creative God; yet the continuity is apparent. Superimposed on (or above) the Greek cosmos is a divine being, creator of all other beings and the font of all order, law, and reason. Though above natural being (and hence above natural reason), however, God provided another means, namely faith and the church, by which men could reflect, in their individual and social lives, that order and level of being through which they achieve happiness, fulfillment, and a meaningful life.

The basic problem of social philosophy for the realist, then, is to determine the place of man and society alongside other beings in the cosmos, in the hierarchical totality of things. This problem depends in turn on that of being and its principles. For its exploration, the work of Aristotle is basic.

What is being? Aristotle noted that this question has many senses, and that the word being is used in many ways. But in its primary meaning, being refers to concrete, individual, existing things such as this desk, this tree, and this man. Aristotle introduced the word substance to refer to beings so understood: desks, trees, and men. Thus far, however, Aristotle did little more than ascribe a new name to things. Much more fundamental is the analysis of what it means to be a substance. Here Aristotle made four observations. First, every substance is made out of something. It derives from something as its constituent basis, as a desk is made of wood. That out of which any thing comes or is made is called its matter or *material cause*. Next, a thing is brought into existence by some power or agency, which is its *efficient cause*. In the case of the desk, a carpenter would be the efficient cause. Third, every thing is characterized as some kind or type of thing, that is, each thing has a distinctive nature which it shares with other things of the same class and which determines that it shall be just that thing and not something else. This is its *formal cause*, which for a desk would be its "deskness." Last is the end or *final cause*. This principle refers to the completed desk for the sake of which the matter, agency, and form are "brought together." While the desk is an artifact produced by human agency, each natural thing belongs to a kind or class, and seeks in itself to become fully and perfectly that kind. Such seeking is for the end which is the completion or perfection of the nature that makes the thing what it is. In fact, the very nature of anything is viewed by Aristotle as a system of capacities or forces of growth directed by the particular nature in question toward the end of completion and full realization of that nature.

This notion of nature and its realization leads to another pair of concepts of great significance for the realist. Viewed simply as a set of capacities tending toward an end, any particular nature is not yet fully being, for it lacks the full realization appropriate to its nature and is, therefore, only *potentially* that completed nature. If a thing does achieve its end, however, it becomes *actual,* that is, most fully a being of its kind. Thus, potentiality is to incomplete as actuality is to complete—the potential involves lack of being; the actual is complete being.

Two technical implications of these concepts must now be noted. The first is the doctrine that being and good are convertible terms. This means that any being, insofar as it is being (that is, has realized its nature), is good, and insofar as it falls short of such realization, it is less than good. For example, a horse is a good horse to the extent that it *is* a horse, that it has realized the nature appropriate to a horse. Or, a man is good as he most fully realizes human nature; he is not good if he fails to do so. To become good is most fully *to be*. The second implication of the concepts of potency and act is the doctrine of the hierarchy of being. This means that beings form an *order of being* by reference to the concepts of potency and act themselves. A thing that is more fully an actuality is higher on the scale of being than a thing that is to some extent or in some respect merely potential, that *is not yet*. The actual is thus prior to the potential. Further, the potential is known by reference to the actual and is actualized by something actual. The not-yet-being becomes being only by the influence of actual being.

The concepts that have been sketched—substance, matter, form, end, potency, act, order, and good—are the instruments with which realists attempt to understand man's social existence and to direct it toward higher ends. Realists form one perspective in social philosophy by the nature of their questions about man and society, by the metaphysical and sometimes religious background and terminology of their position, and by their reliance on the authority of Aristotle. The next task is to turn to the specific positions realists have developed in their social philosophy.

PROBLEM I: MAN AND SOCIETY

The rather abstract discussion of the Introduction may now be given more concrete illustration, for man and society, as beings, are understood by realists through the concepts originally developed by Aristotle. Man, first of all, is a being who has a distinctive nature, namely human nature, that determines the kind of being he is and defines the ends he must realize to become most fully a being. As any person realizes these ends, he achieves "well-being" or happiness. He achieves, in other words, his full being and therewith his good.

This individual human good can be specified more fully, for man is not only a being, he is also a living, animal being and a rational being. As he perfects his animal being with its various desires and appetites, he achieves the *moral virtues* such as courage and temperance, which are the habits of right functioning and realization relative to desires,[3] and as he perfects his rational nature, he realizes such *intellectual virtues* as wisdom, prudence, and art. Happiness, the realist's ethical ideal, is human activity in accordance with virtue; and since his rational nature is unique to him, man is most perfectly fulfilled in the intellectual virtues and the life of contemplation.

[3] The defining mark of "right function" is a mean between the extremes of excess and deficiency. This doctrine is developed below in connection with Aristotle's treatment of justice.

Like all natures, human nature is thus a set of capacities tending toward the distinctively human ends of virtue and happiness. But the virtues are primarily *internal* principles of man's self-realization, and they are not in themselves completely sufficient for happiness. Men stand in need of society in order fully to realize their capacities. And since this need of external conditions is rooted in man's being, it follows that the state or society is natural. The proof of this, as Aristotle said, is that an individual is not self-sufficing when isolated from others; rather, he is like a part in relation to the whole. "A social instinct is implanted in man by nature," and anyone unable to live in society or who has no need of it is either a beast or a god, but not a human being. Men, therefore, cannot be separated from society and the principles of justice and order upon which it depends; they are the parts, society is the whole. Society is the external support of self-realization, and in isolation, men are incapable of becoming rational animals.

It follows for the realist that the state [4] has a moral purpose: "every community is established with a view to some good"; and that, as the individual is to be viewed as a part in relation to the whole, the state is "organic" in structure. The state comes into existence in order that men might live, and it continues in existence for the sake of the good life. Though not itself a substance— states and societies do not have the unity of natural substances— the state has a nature and an end of its own; it is the actuality of less inclusive communities such as the family and the village. The nature of the state requires that it be a proper order under the ideal of justice, that it serve the good of the whole or the common good, that it function according to rules of reason or law, and that the system have a ruling part which acts in trust for the whole community.

[4] The discussion here refers somewhat indiscriminately to either state or society. Most scholars agree that Greek and early medieval thought did not make a distinction between them in any modern way. As Aristotle writes on politics, his thought is directed toward the *polis* or city-state. Modern realists, of course, attempt to relate Aristotle's insights to the modern nation (and democratic) state.

Problem II: Social and Political Values

Man, then, is a social animal. But communities, as Aristotle said at the beginning of the realist tradition, are established with a view to some good—in fact, since the political community is the form or end of all lesser associations, the good at which it aims is the highest and most self-sufficient of human goods.

What is that good? As was noted above in the introduction to realism, the good of anything on realist premises is found in the fulfillment of the being appropriate to the kind of beings one is considering, and then in the "right functioning" or activity of that being. Put another way, good is the fulfillment of proper or natural ends. It follows, then, that communities, societies, social institutions are, for the realist, established to fulfill certain ends, and these ends are not life only, nor companionship, but "noble actions," as Aristotle called them. That is, communities have as their end the provision and maintenance of the external conditions necessary to happiness, to the good and virtuous life.

Of course, not every existing community or state is directed toward this end, and it is therefore possible to say of some states that, since they do not aim for the appropriate good or embody the appropriate values, they are bad societies. Aristotle made the interesting observation that even in such a society one could be a good citizen—one who obeyed rules, customs, and lived for the sake of the society—but one would not thereby be a good man. The goal is to bring together the good of citizenship with the good for man, and this goal can be reached if the proper social ends are realized.

Though realists over the centuries have differed somewhat in the terminology they have used, the principles of peace and justice are generally taken to define the good for society or the common good. Peace, as St. Augustine put it centuries ago, is "the orderly disposal of parts" in society under orderly command and authority, and is the bond which all men desire in their social lives.[5] Justice, which is an ideal to be considered more fully below, is the principle of order that issues forth in peace; its basic definition is "giving everyone his due." Subordinate to these ideals and regulated or distributed by them are two other values, equality and liberty. Equality for realists generally refers to an ideal of equal treatment of all persons under justice, and liberty is the freedom to act rightly according to virtue.[6]

This last observation does not mean that the state with its legal institutions is a moralizing agent in the sense of commanding individual virtue: the proper rule of law in relation to virtue will be explored later. But the social order itself, with its ruling part, is generally viewed by realists as embracing "all the good on earth" (St. Augustine) since it is the highest of human institutions. When state and society embody the essential social and political values, they provide the necessities of life as well as the opportunities for the good life. The state is thus rooted in man's nature and needs, and the values the state seeks to embody are values relative to those needs as the realist understands them.

---

[5] See *The City of God*, tr. John Healy, XII-XV.

[6] The student will want to study carefully the development of concepts of liberty and equality, both in realism and in other perspectives. Though the matter is subject to scholarly debate, there is some agreement that in older political writings one does not find modern conceptions of liberty and equality: not these values, but rather the common good is the highest social principle. Aristotle seemed to deny equality in his theory of "natural slavery," and whether spiritual equality, as in the notion of equality before God, has any political meaning is at least doubtful. Liberty in the sense of conscience, that is, the right to hold, profess, and live by the principles one chooses, first became a social ideal in the toleration controversies of the sixteenth and seventeenth centuries. Whether realistic principles are consistent with recent meanings of liberty and equality is also subject to debate. The student may consult, for example, the social writings of Jacques Maritain or Fr. John C. Murray for efforts made to develop realism in ways sympathetic to these meanings.

PROBLEM III: STATE, POWER, AND AUTHORITY

It has just been observed that society for the realist is a system of ends or purposes rooted in man's nature, where the lower serves the higher and the higher directs the lower. The entire hierarchical structure is controlled by the central values of peace and justice, and the good of the whole is the good of all, or the common good.

Realists make a number of inferences about power and authority from these premises. All power originates in being (for realists who are also theists it originates in the supreme being who is God),[7] is mediated through the people in the community, and is entrusted to some ruler. The common good itself dictates that there be some head or ruling part upon whom the order and structure of society centers. Rulership is a trust for the whole community that seeks to lay the foundations of human happiness by maintaining peace and order. Furthermore, the moral purpose of government implies that authority must be limited and exercised only in accordance with law. Law, the subject of the next section, makes for legitimate government, and the common good makes for its necessity.

Thus, the basic realist view of government is that of a central authority which acts for the common good and which is morally justified by the fact that it is lawful. But what form should actual governments take? In his *Politics*, Aristotle distinguished monarchy, aristocracy, and polity as legitimate forms of government, and gave tyranny, oligarchy, and democracy as the parallel corruptions of each.[8] This classification is based primarily on a quantitative principle: rule by one, by a few, or by many. Aristotle himself expressed

[7] See also *Romans* 13:1: "For there is no power but of God: the powers that be are ordained of God."

[8] "Democracy" for Greek thinkers did not have its modern meaning; it rather connoted "mob-rule." The legitimate forms are marked by the rule of law and the common good, the corruptions by the absence of these factors.

a preference for a "mixed" government, though he recognized that the varying circumstances of different peoples might dictate different governmental forms. One-man rule allows for unity and decisiveness, the rule of an elite allows for the selection of the best abilities in the state, and the rule of polity or constitutional democracy allows for freedom and economic equality. Medieval realists on the whole preferred monarchy, for they saw an analogy between God's rule of creation and the king's rule of his kingdom. Modern realists have generally argued for polity of some form or other. Important as the question of the form of government is—and it is important for the realist, since the aim of statecraft is to develop a form and ethos that will synthesize the historic conditions of a people with basic political values—it is nevertheless subordinate to questions of legitimacy through law and moral purpose.

Given its long period of historical development, realism understandably found expression in the medieval as well as in the ancient world. Some reference to important medieval thinkers supplies background for contemporary realist theories of the state and may well be of interest in themselves. The first representative is John of Salisbury (c. 1120–1180), who wrote after Pope Gelasius (492–496) had developed the doctrine of two authorities, one spiritual and one temporal. The conflicts between papacy and empire that continued through the Middle Ages were developing in John's time, and he generally sided with the papists in these controversies. His position, however, allowed him to hold three important views. He believed that the authority of the papacy would provide a check on unjust and intemperate temporal rulers. He developed—quite independently of Aristotle's thought, which he did not know—an organic conception of society. His famous analogy of society and the human body points out the dependence of parts on the whole, which is the essential feature of organic theories of the state. The analogy also points out the dependence of lower parts of the head, which is the principle of hierarchy. Finally, John inferred the right of tyrannicide, which term provided the medieval context for what today is usually referred to as the problem of civil disobedience. A king, he believed, is distinguished from a tyrant as law is from force, and tyrants may be slain if it becomes necessary to rid the body politic of their evil influence. In this doctrine John went far beyond other medieval thinkers, who generally denied the right of tyrannicide altogether or limited it only to subordinate officials, not to the people as a whole.

The second representative, Marsilius of Padua (1275–1343), stands historically as a link between the medieval and modern periods as well as between realism and later developments in social philosophy.[9] Following Aristotle, Marsilius defined the state as a kind of "living being" composed of parts that perform functions necessary to its life. The health of the social organism is expressed in the orderly working of its parts and in the peace that issues from such order. Such an idea has been met in preceding sections.

But Marsilius added a further and distinctive notion to this idea, for he taught that good governments rule for the benefit of the people *with their consent*. This doctrine was by no means discovered by Marsilius; it was commonly held from Greek and Roman days by philosophers and statesmen alike that the people are the source of authority. To be sure, such consent was not equivalent to the modern idea of "popular sovereignty." Rather, it was most frequently connected with the notion of custom,[10] for kingship was believed to be both legitimate and based on consent if it existed for a relatively long time. While he did not discover this teaching, Marsilius cleared it of all encumbrances so that it could become a call to action. He also integrated this teaching and the process of election, another idea from Aristotle. Marsilius took election to be the most certain standard of government, and his full position is that the basis of authority is the will of the community as expressed in election.

[9] The student may follow this on two points at least. Marsilius looks forward historically to positivist and utilitarian doctrines in his view that law is not derived from divine law, as St. Thomas Aquinas for example believed, but is rather the commands of the legislator enforceable in the courts. The practical meaning of this definition is that the teaching of priests has no proper power or (political) authority. Secondly, there is much in Marsilius that anticipates the modern secular state, such as his belief that in order to insure peace, the papacy must be denied authority in temporal affairs.

[10] Some authorities, in fact, hold that the ancient political distinction between "nature" and "convention" might better be expressed as "custom" and "convention."

Much of the writing of John and Marsilius must be seen in the light of the conflicts and problems of their day. To some extent also, Marsilius is a transitional figure who clearly expressed Aristotelian realism, and yet looked beyond the political forms of his day. Contemporary realists, of course, face the political forms of the modern world, dominated as it is by the idea of the nation-state and by political alternatives such as democracy, socialism, and communism. To be sure, realists (like other philosophers) do not always agree in their political judgments, that is, judgments about the right means to appropriate social ends. Still, there is agreement on the ends: the good state aims at such values as peace and justice, its authority is made legitimate through the consent of the governed, and its operations are conducted according to laws which respect the natural law and promote natural rights.

Problem IV: Law and Rights

The pivot of realistic social philosophy is the doctrine of natural law, and even today the major text for its exposition is the "Treatise on Law" in St. Thomas Aquinas' *Summa Theologica*. A long tradition lay behind his work: Aristotle stated fundamental realistic assumptions about law and justice in his ethical and political writings, Cicero spelled out even more the belief in law as right reason embodied in the very structure of the universe, and Stoic lawyers of Rome continued to develop and amplify the position. Aquinas drew heavily on these many sources, yet much is original in his view of law. He is generally less dependent on Aristotle here than in other aspects of his social doctrine. Contemporary realists have amplified Thomistic views as new problems and circumstances have arisen. But the fundamental outlook on law remains for most realists Thomistic.

Aquinas (1226–1274) invited his reader to take a start, not with the individual and so-called individual rights, but rather with the cosmos, that is, with the conception of a world well-ordered and graded by rational principle. There is an order of being, under

God, who is the primal Being, in which man can participate through his rationality. The very being of God expresses itself in rationality and providential concern over creation, instructing rational creatures (man) by law and assisting them by grace. Aquinas calls this law of God eternal law; the other levels of law that will concern us are most properly law only as they reflect or participate in the eternal law itself.

But what is law? Aquinas defined it as a rule and measure of acts that induces or restrains a man's activity. He noted immediately, however, that reason is the source of all command, and he inferred next that law pertains to reason. Law, in fact, is reason measuring actions. Thus, reason is the extrinsic principle of acts (virtue is their intrinsic principle), and rules not in accord with reason are not properly laws at all.

Three levels of law are specified in Aquinas' social philosophy.[11] The first and highest law, namely eternal law, has been mentioned above. Eternal law is imprinted on creatures; from it they derive their inclinations to their proper ends and acts. Since man participates in rationality, this imprinted law can be apprehended by him and thus is itself a law rooted in and appropriate to his nature. Aquinas called it the natural law; the law that rules and measures actions with special reference to the nature of man. When considered simply as a being, man is directed to such ends as are common to all beings, such as self-preservation. When considered as an animal being, man is directed toward procreation and the education of offspring. As a human being, he is given, for example, the desire to know God.

The natural law, Aquinas taught, is directed toward the common good and universal happiness. As with all law, it thus aims to lead men to that fulfillment of being or nature which is the good. Whatever is prescribed or prohibited by natural law is done so with reference to the attainment of the ends of human nature under the guidance of reason. Reason itself, Aquinas noted, is a reflection of being, and acts of virtue are dictates of reason. It therefore follows that, in this sense, natural law commands all

---

[11] A fourth type of law, divine law, is also explored by Aquinas. This law is primarily religious in character, in the sense that it is addressed to man's quest for salvation, and curbs and directs *interior* human acts.

the acts of virtue [12] and, since reason and man's being are every-where and always the same, the natural law is identical for all men in its common principles and unchangeable in its content except by addition.

Finally, Aquinas recognized a third level of law, namely human or positive [13] law. Perfection in virtue, he argued, requires training and control, together with the restraints of force and fear. Laws, therefore, must be framed by human societies to achieve the order and peace needed for perfection. Human law is also needed to order the particular practices of societies that differ from one another, and even the particular conclusions of the natural law may differ from one people to another, according to Aquinas. But in all its detailed developments, human law is truly law only as it is derived from the natural law.

Correlative with natural law is the doctrine of natural rights. A right, generally, is a power or privilege which the law grants and guarantees to the individual, and rights may be viewed as the other side of the legal coin. Natural rights in a realist philosophy, like the natural law, are the guarantees for individuals believed rooted in our essential nature, in our *humanitas*.[14] In specifying natural rights, realists have generally followed Aristotle's basic understanding of human nature. Thus, when man is considered simply as a being, he has such natural rights as the integrity of his body (for example, freedom from mutilation). As a living being, he has a right to life and to the necessities of life. As an animal or desiring being, he has such natural rights as to live under a just economic system and to a just wage. Finally, as a rational, spiritual being, man has the natural rights of freedom of conscience and the worship of God. This listing is, of course, illustrative only, and

---

[12] Though it does not command all virtuous acts considered in themselves. Aquinas distinguished private from public virtues, and wrote that "human law does not prescribe concerning all the acts of every virtue: but only in regard to those that ordained to the common good." *Summa Theologica*, I-II, Q. 96.

[13] This is the more customary term in recent discussions of the law.

[14] This essentialist view of natural rights can be contrasted with the individual-istic approach derived from the philosophy of John Locke (see Chapter Three). An important study of these two alternatives is found in Edward S. Corwin, *The "Higher Law" Background of American Constitutional Law*, Ithaca, 1955.

states may also grant positive rights through enactment of human or positive laws.

The theory of natural law has a central position in realist philosophy. It looks back, so to speak, to fundamental assumptions about being, man, nature, and the good. At the same time it looks forward, for natural law serves as the basis upon which realists make judgments on further problems in social philosophy such as obligation and specific issues requiring political decision. The importance of this theory is reflected in realist writings to the present day.

Problem V: Political Obligation

The problem of political obligation as understood in the modern world is in many ways a new concern. The philosophic assumptions of realism as well as the social conditions of the Greek city-state and medieval feudalism did not lead to the formulation of distinct questions regarding the grounds of political obligation. These questions had to wait the great change between the Middle Ages and the modern era, and the latter age developed the concept of a central and supreme sovereign within the state to whom every person owes allegiance.

But the emphasis must be on "distinct questions," for there is certainly implicit in realist writing, traditional and contemporary alike, a theory of political obligation. By nature man is a social animal because society is necessary to his very being, both in making life possible and the good life available. The obligations to live in society and to accept the conditions necessary to the existence of society such as order, authority, and government thus derive from man's very being and his need to fulfill that being.

The need for society is a fact of man's nature. What gives it moral legitimacy? Why should men feel obliged to accept regulation and authority? Because, realists answer, the fulfillment of man's being is itself a moral obligation and because society, when directed toward the common good and ordered by natural law,

serves as the external ground and support of that fulfillment. The
* basis of political obligation is the nature of man; the state has its
roots in social experience which shows that a governing authority
is necessary for order; and natural law determines the legitimacy
and scope of political authority: these assertions are the core of
the realistic understanding of the political obligation that every
citizen has to the state. But these same assumptions imply that
the state, in turn, has obligations to its citizens. The ideas of
natural law, justice, and the common good mean that government
must be directed by reference to duties and limitations. Law and
the common good are, for realists, the grounds on which political
relations are secured, comprehended, and made legitimate and
obligatory.

√ Realists thus view society as ordered interactions between
governed and governor, teleologically directed toward man's happiness. Should an individual citizen violate the common good by
breaking the law, thereby destroying these relations, the state
properly has the right to judge and punish, even to restrain the
offender, so as to maintain order. On the question of transgressions
by the state, however, realists have differed widely. John of Salisbury, as was observed above, taught a doctrine of tyrannicide, but
his views are not generally shared by other realists. Aquinas is
perhaps more representative of medieval realism in his denial that
the people as a whole have the right to depose a tyrant. This right
falls only to those who share in political authority such as lesser
officials of the realm. Through the centuries since Aquinas, realists
have tended to waver between these two views.

The contemporary form of the question regarding transgressions of justice by the state is in terms of the right of civil disobedience. Civil disobedience is generally understood as an act of
law breaking; but unlike crime, it is (1) directed toward some end
believed necessary under an ideal of justice, (2) public rather than
covert, (3) motivated by a desire to improve society as a whole,
even if the sought-for justice is particularly important to a special
group, and (4) practiced with a willingness to accept the punishment that might be given for the disobedience. There is, to be
sure, always a practical problem connected with any proposed act
of civil disobedience. Will the act accomplish, or best accomplish,

the ends sought? But apart from this judgment, realists who accept civil disobedience as a means to change do so on the basis of the very same principle which grounds obedience, namely, the proper ends ordained for society and the state. Civil disobedience finds a justification in principle in such ideals as justice, peace, natural law, and natural rights, however much realist philosophers may agree or disagree over the wisdom of particular acts of disobedience.

Problem VI: The Ideal of Justice

Reflection on the meaning of justice has ancient roots, and almost from the beginning of philosophy, thinkers were concerned with it. Pre-Socratic philosophers like Heraclitus (536–470) wrote of parallels between the law of the world and the law of society. Possibly this thought also occurred to Anaximander (sixth century), one of his predecessors. The school of Pythagoras (572–497) went further in articulating the meaning of justice. Justice, they said, is a number multiplied by itself, that is, a square number. A square number is a perfect harmony because it is composed of equal parts. It follows, therefore, that justice is related to a conception of the state based on equal parts. The Pythagoreans also defined justice as requital, for it is the measure between aggressor and loser in acts of injustice.

Influenced by the Pythagoreans, Plato articulated further the ideal of justice in terms of harmony and measure, and he believed that justice and law are the common spiritual substance of a society that bring and hold it together. He understood justice in terms of an adjustment that gives the parts or factors forming a society their proper place, for the justice of a society is the citizen's sense of the duties of his station in that society. From his station, the citizen discharges his appropriate function in public action. While this conception of justice is a principle of social ethics that gives coherence to the community as a whole, it served Plato as an ideal of individual ethics as well. In fact, Plato quite deliberately compared society and the individual, holding that both are made of parts or elements, that both demand meaningful unification, and that both ought to be ordered by reason in the light of the ideal of justice.

The dominant philosophical trend of Greece to which these allusions refer provided the background for Aristotle's more detailed treatment of justice.[15] Justice, he wrote, is fairness in human action, and fairness is a mean between the extremes of excess and deficiency, of too much and too little.[16] Justice therefore is a mean; it involves the fair or equal and, as justice involves persons and their relations, it is relative to certain persons.

These references to fairness, equality, and the mean indicate that Aristotle understood justice as the principle of coherence and order in society. As he specified the conception of justice further, his emphasis on rational order is even more apparent, for he related justice to mathematical principles. Distributive or social justice is based on the notion of geometrical proportion: it is defined as a mean between the violations of proportion. Corrective justice, which seeks to restore equality by imposing penalties, is based on arithmetical proportion, and is a mean between the extremes of "profit" and "loss." All actions involving injustice damage or destroy the coherence of society because they aim at the destructive extreme.[17]

The influence of Aristotle's views on justice, on philosophy generally, and on later theories of realism in particular can hardly be exaggerated. There have been, it is true, additions and modifications of the doctrine, but Aristotle gave it its fundamental meaning and direction. Realistic assumptions about man and society, as they

[15] Though much of Greek thought was realistic, in part or by way of anticipation, the student should not infer that realism was the sole position in the philosophy of that time. Quite the opposite is the case, for the adventurous Greek mind touched on many of the chief alternatives in social philosophy.

[16] Aristotle also used the idea of the mean to define the moral virtues. Courage, for example, is the mean between the excesses of foolhardiness on the one hand, and cowardice on the other.

[17] Aristotle also introduced the principle of equity, largely to treat of individual cases and "correct" legal justice. The reason for this correction is that law must be universal, "but about some things it is not possible to make a universal statement which shall be correct." See the *Nicomachean Ethics*, V, 10.

have been suggested in previous sections, provide the context in which the ideal of justice takes on its full meaning: happiness as the fulfillment of man's being, society as a moral and educational organism, and order and authority as conditions of happiness. Perhaps most basic of all, however, is the realist's belief that, though men come to recognize the need of society out of a variety of motives, "the ultimate bond of human society is reason." [18]

Bibliographical Essay

Systematic introductions to classical realism are given in such volumes as Jacques Maritain, *An Introduction to Philosophy*, London, 1930; and John Wild, *Introduction to Realistic Philosophy*, New York, 1948. For further intensive study, the student must turn to the basic texts of the great figures in classical realism—Plato, Aristotle, and St. Thomas Aquinas. Their works are available in many editions and compilations. Of value in studying them are commentaries by Jacques Maritain, *Saint Thomas Aquinas*, London, 1933; W. D. Ross, *Aristotle*, 5th ed., London, 1949; F. C. Copleston, *Aquinas*, Harmondsworth, England, 1955; Étienne Gilson, *The Christian Philosophy of St. Thomas Aquinas*, New York, 1956; A. E. Taylor, *Plato, the Man and His Work*, 4th ed., New York, 1956; G. M. A. Grube, *Plato's Thought*, Boston, 1958; and Robert S. Brumbaugh, *Plato for the Modern Age*, New York, 1962. Sir Ernest Barker's work on Plato and Aristotle, as well as relevant books mentioned above, are also helpful on the social philosophy of the important figures in realism. A recent study is R. G. Mulgen, *Aristotle's Political Theory*, Oxford, 1978. Many books exist on the history of realism; see, for example, Maurice de Wulf, *History of Medieval Philosophy*, New York, 1909; the interpretative and excellent study by Gilson, *The Spirit of Medieval Philosophy*, New York, 1940; and Émile Bréhier, *The Middle Ages and the Renaissance*, trans. Wade Baskin, Chicago, 1965. The thought of such

[18] Étienne Gilson, *The Christian Philosophy of St. Thomas Aquinas*, trans. L. K. Shook, New York, 1956, p. 327.

figures as John of Salisbury and Marsilius is covered in histories of social philosophy; see also John Dickinson's translation of *The Statesman's Book of John of Salisbury*, New York, 1927, and Alan Gewirth's translation of Marsilius' *The Defender of Peace*, New York, 1956. Contemporary work by thinkers of a realistic persuasion is found in such volumes as John Wild (ed.), *The Return to Reason*, Chicago, 1953, the *Proceedings of the American Catholic Philosophic Association*, and the many publications of Gilson and Maritain, who have written on all the major fields of philosophical concern.

References in the chapter have frequently been given to ancient and medieval realistic sources. While relying on these sources, contemporary realists have attempted to restate older insights in ways relevant to the modern world. Widely read have been such writings of Jacques Maritain as *True Humanism*, New York, 1938, *Scholasticism and Politics*, New York, 1940, and *The Person and the Common Good*, New York, 1947. Other works include A. P. d'Entrèves, *Natural Law: An Introduction to Legal Philosophy*, London, 1951, and *The Notion of the State*, Oxford, 1967; Yves Simon, *The Tradition of Natural Law: A Philosopher's Reflections*, New York, 1965; and John Wild, *Plato's Modern Enemies and the Theory of Natural Law*, Chicago, 1953. Henry Veatch's *Rational Man*, Bloomington, 1962, is a stirring defense of Aristotelian principles. Journals especially to be consulted include *International Philosophical Quarterly*, *The Thomist*, *The Modern Schoolman*, and *The New Scholasticism*.

CHAPTER 2

Positivism 2

It is often pointed out that the word positivism has been used in two ways: to name a particular philosophy and to stand for a distinctive, but rather common, temper of mind. In its first meaning, positivism is historically associated with the eccentric yet influential French philosopher, Auguste Comte (1798–1857), who was the first thinker to use the word for a philosophical position. This use is connected with his famous "law" of social growth and with the evaluation of different modes of knowledge implicit in it.

All history, Comte taught, passes through three different ascending levels.[1] The most primitive is the *theological*, where men attempt to explain natural phenomena by appealing to spiritual, anthropomorphic beings. The second stage, the *metaphysical*, depersonalizes these beings so that they become forces and essences. The third level is the *positive*, where explanation proceeds by scientific description. Correlative with these stages in knowledge are different organizations of society and the highest of these, according to Comte, is that which is based firmly on science and scientific discoveries.[2]

Comte's philosophy leads to and is included in the second meaning of positivism as a special temper of mind. Most broadly put, this attitude involves a "tough-minded" orientation toward facts and natural phenomena. It holds that thought should confine

---

[1] Comte referred to this law in many places, among them, for example, *The Positive Philosophy*, trans. Harriet Martineau, New York, 1855.

[2] Comte's views on these matters are treated further below.

itself to the data of experience and reject all transcendent meta-physical and abstract speculation. So understood, positivism has been a recurring position in the history of thought, represented by a stream of philosophers from the Sophists of ancient Greece to contemporary analytic positivists. But thus understood, the term may be so broad that the student will find it of little or no value since it will apply to many quite divergent philosophies, and its meaning for social philosophy will be vague, if not completely lost. While taking the fact-orientation of the positivist as a starting point, therefore, one must specify the themes of positivism more closely in order to make the term a useful classificatory device. This can be done by examining more carefully typical positivist theories of *knowledge*, of *value*, and of *society*.

1. Positivism in the more technical sense may be character-ized, first, by its claim that science provides man with the clearest possible ideal of knowledge. Rejecting theological, metaphysical, and speculative methods, the positivist argues that phenomena—social as well as natural—are to be explained by scientific laws, not by ends, final causes or transcendent grounds. Speculation is to be replaced by science, wisdom becomes control through science, and philosophy, in its traditional sense, is judged to be a meaning-less, if not a dangerous illusion.

These assertions are perhaps clear enough, but the student should watch for several refinements of them. It must be noted that, except for a few sporadic anticipations (Machiavelli, for example, in social thought), positivism arose with the scientific revolution of the seventeenth century. Historians usually place the rise of modern science in that century (only organic chemistry had to await a later date), and the century's philosophers such as Bacon, Descartes, Leibniz, and Locke articulated the methods and as-sumptions on which science rests.

Next, the student should watch for various conceptions of science and for their distinctive elements. Different men during different times have practiced science diversely, and they have also interpreted and applied science in quite divergent ways. Hobbes, for example, viewed science as a deductive procedure that begins with adequate definitions and proceeds by demonstration of derived consequences. Saint-Simon, Comte, and the "scientific socialists" of the nineteenth century understood science to be the formulation of descriptive generalizations (laws) derived from uninterpreted and unbiased observation. Modern science has yet another emphasis, employing chiefly though not solely the hypothesis that may be described briefly as "hypothetical-deductive." To understand a social philosopher who takes science to be his model or ideal of knowledge, it is necessary to grasp something of his conception of science.

Another caution concerns the relation of science to philosophy in different philosophic perspectives. Positivists are not alone in attempting to relate science to philosophy; modern philosophers of all persuasions face this problem. Positivists are not alone either in seeking to *base* philosophy on science; in their own ways, utilitarians, Marxists, and pragmatists do the same.[3] The main point is that the embrace of science is a fundamental element in positivism, though it is not alone the principal characteristic.

(2.) Consistent with its orientation toward fact, positivism rejects all attempts to understand value in metaphysical and non-empirical ways. Statements about the convertibility of being and good and about the rational order of value are examples of speculative assertions that the positivist finds to be nonsense. Not that the positivist thinks values are unimportant to men; he rather believes that value must be understood within the context of human life and in ways susceptible to scientific treatment. Positivists have often defined value in a noncognitive yet empirical way—as need or interest, for example—and have analyzed rules of value as imperatives or commands to men to behave in certain ways. Even for positivists like Comte, who wrote about developing a "science of value," the emphasis is on observable needs and on generalizations regarding the means for satisfying these needs.

(3.) This noncognitive yet empirical understanding of value may be amplified and illustrated by reference to society. The starting point of this approach is not man's moral needs such as the realization of virtue (as, for example, in realism), but needs in the

---

[3] The differences are important however. Positivists generally have been influenced by the procedures of physics, pragmatists by biology, utilitarians seek to give morals and legislation a scientific status, and Marxists offer a scientific law of history.

form of desires and interests. At times these needs have been viewed in terms of self-assertion (Machiavelli) and security (Hobbes), at other times in terms of a variety of satisfactions of wants (Comte). But the main effort of positivists is to look empirically at human nature and social conduct in order to isolate the basic needs of individuals living together in the context of cooperation and mutual dependence. In this context human beings also develop rules and standards governing their associative lives, and positivists believe that these too are subject to scientific investigation. Thus, to illustrate: moral value, which involves relations of persons to each other, may be understood empirically as obedience to positive law or custom, and justice is found in the concrete workings of society and government rather than in the realm of transcendent ideals.

These assertions, then, serve as an introduction to positivist thought: the primacy of science and the rejection of metaphysics, an empirical theory of value, and an understanding of man and society in terms of human needs and interests. Their fuller meaning and implications for social philosophy are developed in the sections that follow.

PROBLEM I: MAN AND SOCIETY

Thomas Hobbes (1588–1679) is the first great thinker to attempt to bring political philosophy into relationship with a modern system of ideas. Scorning Aristotle's "essences" and definitions based on purposes, he sought to accomplish in political theory what scientists were achieving in physics and cosmology. While his view of science has been out of date for a long time, he did produce something of a "science of politics."

Hobbes attempted to explain man and society solely in terms of self-interest, without reference to transcendent sanctions or metaphysical notions like the common good.[4] Realists and other natural law theorists argue that society must preserve the basic

[4] See especially Hobbes' *Leviathan*, available in many editions and reprints.

moral conditions of civilized life, and that these conditions are determined by reference to ends or purposes. Hobbes asserted that causes, not ends, control human life, and that a scientific account of causes will lead to an understanding of society. Thus rejecting final causes, Hobbes proceeded in Cartesian [5] fashion to frame clear and real definitions and to develop their implications deductively.

Considered in themselves and apart from society (that is, in the "state of nature"), men are fundamentally equal. In matters of strength, of ability, and of hope for attaining their own ends, there is no basic difference among them that requires special attention in political theory. The last quality especially, namely hope, which is shared by all men, is the source of the misery pervading the natural state of man; from it arises the desire of domination over others to secure one's own interests. Men quarrel or "war" with each other from motives of competition, difference or fear, and glory; the natural condition of men is thus a state of war of man against man. Life is solitary, poor, nasty, brutish, and short.

What men desire, Hobbes is saying, is what they call good, and happiness is success in getting what is desired. And since all men are equal and motivated in the same way, each man finds that his hopes, values, and happiness are threatened and insecure. The state of nature does not offer hope for security. Since there is no law, there is no common power that all men fear and obey, and there are no constraining notions of morality or justice. Hobbes used the traditional terms, natural right and natural law, of the state of nature, but he emptied them of all traditional meaning. Natural right is the liberty of each man to use his power to preserve himself, and natural laws are rules of conduct given by reason for the sake of one's own interests. In neither case, however, did Hobbes intend to write of normative moral principles. Even as he wrote of natural law, he believed he was only describing the condition of man and the causes that account for his behavior.

Since man's natural condition is one of misery, Hobbes inferred that it is in man's interest to form societies and governments. The need for security leads to a demand for common power, and

[5] René Descartes (1596–1650), a French philosopher and one of the developers of the theory of scientific method. Incidentally, it may be noted that Spinoza applied the Cartesian method morally, Hobbes in a nonmoral fashion.

since the state of nature is essentially without effective power and
obligation, even a modest need for security leads to an endless
need of power. Therefore, men consent to the creation of a
sovereign power who can secure their interests by removing the
threats to them in the state of nature. Further, Hobbes argued,
wherever power is effective, it is to man's advantage to submit to
it. The act of consent, the "social contract," is kept because it is
in the interest of every man; rules limiting obedience to government are never in the interest of man. To submit to power is to
consent to it, and consent creates the duty of obedience in the
sense that the ruler who maintains such security—since men have
more to gain than lose by submission to him—acquires the right
of command. With command comes law and with law justice,
morality, and civilization.

For Hobbes, sovereign power is the only basis for an effective
society and government.[6] To be sure, men are not naturally inclined
to society; they have to be prepared for it by education. Yet sovereignty, justice, and honesty, and indeed all political behavior,
are but refined forms of egoism, for they were understood by
Hobbes always to contain a reference to self-interest. Beyond
separate self-interests, Hobbes admits no explanatory principles.
Society itself is an "artificial" body, for the word itself refers only
to the fact that human beings find it individually advantageous to
exchange goods and services and to submit to control.

There is another side of Hobbes' position which deserves
special mention and which is of great importance in contemporary
philosophy. This is the problem of human action. Seeking explanations of all phenomena in terms of causes, Hobbes and his succes-
sors have argued that human behavior results, not from occult
antecedents or unempirical realities like soul or consciousness, or
even subjectively held reasons, but from real and observable social
determinants. This means that men do not act to create the social
conditions of their lives but that they are rather determined and
molded in their actions and very characters by the society in which
they live. Much of the discovery and analysis of these social forces
is the work of social scientists—philosophy for positivists is more

6 Hobbes took society and government finally to mean the same thing. Any
distinction between them, as any between law and morals, is confusion.

an analysis of meaning than a discovery of facts—although philosophical movements like scientific socialism and Marxism, which
aim to be scientific, have based themselves on a purported law of
society or history.[7]

This understanding of society and human action has also led
to the concept of "social engineering" as represented, for example,
in the work of B. F. Skinner.[8] Skinner's position rests on the two
theses that human behavior is the consequence of antecedent and
causal social factors, and that these factors can be altered to change
human behavior, even to achieve a utopian vision. The model of
humanity which these theses entail has been suggestively named
"Plastic Man."[9]

In these accomplishments Hobbes remains for many social
scientists, as A. D. Lindsay said, "the father of us all." Contemporary efforts in political science, sociology, and economics to find
explanatory social principles in terms of egoism or rational self-
interest, of needs for security, or of institutional and power
relations remain indebted to the work of Hobbes. Theoretical
refinements in these social sciences have departed from many of
the details of Hobbes' theories, but in them is found one of the
motivations for the effort to develop the social sciences.

Problem II: Social and Political Values

What can men do who, without reference to theology and
metaphysics, want to explain society and its values as a complex

---

[7] Some of the major alternative views in action theory are conveniently anthologized in Myles Brand (ed.), *The Nature of Human Action*, Glenview,
Ill., 1970.

[8] See *Walden Two*, New York, 1948, and *Beyond Freedom and Dignity*,
London, 1973. Similar views suggesting versions of social engineering are
touched on below in the chapters on Utilitarianism, Communism, and
Pragmatism.

[9] In, for example, Martin Hollis, *Models of Man*, Cambridge, 1977.

structure adapted to men's needs? As we have seen, Hobbes' answer
was in terms of science, understood primarily as a matter of definition and deduction. By the end of the eighteenth century,
however, there was a developing realization that science relies
on observation and induction rather than deduction. Hence
arose the necessity for those influenced by the general positivist temper to rethink the meanings of science, philosophy, and
social value.

One important source of this reexamination and construction
is the work of Saint-Simon and his followers. Comte de Saint-
Simon (1760–1825) maintained the positivist conviction that everything happens according to laws that can be known by observation
and experiment. The Saint-Simonians held that a scientific explanation of society could be found by postulating a law of historical change on the basis of induction. This they did, Comte
offering his famous law of three stages,[10] and Saint-Simon himself
devising a principle of the alternation of organic and critical
periods of history. Such "laws" of society and history, whether
formulated in the past or in some contemporary form, have provided positivist philosophers and social scientists with what they
believe to be an explanation of historical process, an understanding
of the goal of historical movement, and a grasp of the values that
society is gradually seeking to embody.

Saint-Simon's law is one of progress from organic to critical
periods of social organization, and back to organic ones; the goal
of history is an organic period of universal association. An organic
society is one whose purposes are clearly defined for all its members and which, therefore, is harmonious and unified. A critical
period, which involves criticism and destruction of forms of order,
leads to anarchy and egoism. The recurring cycle of organic and
critical stages tends ultimately toward an organic society which,
unlike such societies in the past, will be universal and based on
science.

The world, the Saint-Simonians said, is on the threshold of a

---

[10] See the introduction to positivism above. Comte remained a disciple of
Saint-Simon for a while, but later broke with the master.

new organic age. The developing industrial society will become organic when it is given a positive purpose, by which is meant not just a common notion of justice but a general sharing in a common enterprise. That enterprise, to be accomplished when society is scientifically organized, is the multiplication and satisfaction of human wants. That is, society should be taken over by industrialists who, supported by scientists and artists, would manage its resources as means to human satisfactions. Government would become primarily the seat of administration rather than the center of organized force (many early socialists felt that if their reforms were adopted, the need for force to maintain order would greatly diminish), it would be in the hands of experts, and it would be directed, even made possible, by scientific knowledge and techniques. So understood, universal association is the final goal of history, not as some static state of perfection, but as a society organized directly for progress. The law of history is in fact also a law of progress: the evidence for progress is empirical, and the reason for progress is causal.[11]

Thus the Saint-Simonians held satisfaction through science rather than through liberty or equality to be the primary social value. Impressed more by how science affects man's conception of his world than by particular developments, they defined philosophy as a kind of compendium of the sciences, including the new science of sociology that they as well as Comte had promoted. They believed that philosophy so conceived would do for an industrial society what theology had done for feudal society, namely to give it a cosmology intimately connected with a morality suitable for the age. Philosophy, society, morality—even man's very nature —are all under the control and spirit of the scientific enterprise and the values it contains or discovers. The positivist emphasis, present as well as past, maintains this belief in the centrality of scientific understanding and the necessity of achieving social progress through application of scientific insights.

11 As is the case with many positivists, the Saint-Simonians also coupled this belief with a theory of social determinism, for they held that the way men behave is determined by their society and culture.

Problem III: State, Power, and Authority

Though fascinating and important to all political theorists, questions of power and authority have been particularly central for many positivists. The reason for this is not difficult to see, for while there are other possible candidates, power appears as the most striking observable fact about social organization. Whether one considers the structure and parts of government, the authority of law, or the effects of rule, one finds a factor common to them all. This, many positivists assert, is power. And since power and its effects are observable, an account of the state in terms of power will provide both a theory of social behavior and a social philosophy free of unempirical speculation.

Two classic examples of this approach are found in the writings of Machiavelli (1469–1527) [12] and Bodin (1530–1596). One of the most representative men of the Italian Renaissance, Machiavelli warned his reader that he intended to say something useful about government, and that to this end he will go to the truth of the matter, not to imagination. "The manner in which we live," he wrote, "and that in which we ought to live, are things so wide asunder, that he who quits the one to betake himself to the other is more likely to destroy than to save himself." Machiavelli's interest is in man in his political behavior; man is political not as a being capable of realizing his potentialities in society, but as a lover of power and reputation, as self-assertive in wishing to control others.

Machiavelli thus considered the state as many modern thinkers do. He did not view it as a hierarchy of magistrates whose authority is defined by custom or as a *polis* or a commonwealth aiming at the moral development of its citizens and preserving them from

---

[12] Machiavelli's most widely read book is *The Prince*, available in many different editions.

evil. Rather, the state is a human contrivance, morally neutral, organized for power, and centered in a single, all-controlling structure. Machiavelli rejected the idea common to many theories that there is an end for society for which power is a means. He made power an end in itself, and suggested an autonomous system of "values" implied by this end. In relation to power, the good becomes efficiency (hence Machiavelli's oft-debated nonmoralism), and morality and justice, in their more ordinary meanings, are acquired by men only by living in a society. For Machiavelli morality and even religion are subservient to the rules of power, which override all other considerations. The advice of his very influential book, *The Prince*, is indoctrination into these rules of power.

Machiavelli's approach to politics cannot be called scientific in any modern sense, for he knew nothing of the experimental method or of disciplined classification of facts. But he certainly is positivist in spirit in his factual temper and his use of shrewd common sense. Perhaps the most striking feature of all, however, is his secularism, with its rather total absence of any moral framework for the state. This does not mean, of course, that Machiavelli had no preference for society. He believed that, for the preservation of liberty, popular government is best for a vigorous and healthy people, and he spoke of *virtu* as the energy of the patriotic and valuable citizen. Yet Machiavelli always believed that the first condition of order and liberty is the preservation or enlargement of power, and he was prepared, if necessary, to support even a tyrant to achieve the needed power.

A second classical view is found in the important discussion of sovereignty by the French theorist, Jean Bodin.[13] By sovereignty Bodin meant the perpetual, humanly unlimited, and unconditional right to make, interpret, and execute law; "the absolute and perpetual power in a commonwealth." Though he remained more medieval than Machiavelli, with whom he is often compared, Bodin agreed that politics should be studied on the basis of experience, and that the state should be explained by itself rather than from

[13] See Bodin's *Six Books of the Commonwealth*, trans. M. J. Tooley, Oxford, 1955.

some supposed metaphysical or divinely given order of the universe. Bodin also agreed with both Hobbes and Machiavelli that sovereign power is the only basis for effective government.

Bodin himself did not derive the notion of limitless power from the sovereign's supreme legal authority—others were to do this later. Sovereignty remained for him the unlimited power of making law, which he defined as the command of the sovereign touching all his subjects on general matters. Natural law, the law of succession, and the right to private property were limits on power accepted by Bodin. Unlike some positivists, Bodin was also interested in questions of the legitimacy of government, although he did not distinguish this moral issue from questions of fact. Nevertheless, the doctrine of sovereignty is historically a most influential conception, involving as it does the explicit rejection of medieval ideas about the limited authority of the state and of unempirical efforts to understand its functions.[14]

Problem IV: Law and Rights

The positivist approach to problems of law and jurisprudence is the same as that developed in the preceding sections of this part: positivists seek solutions to these problems by the methods of science, and the shift is from metaphysical methods to empirical ones. This general statement can be made more specific, however, for the adjective "positivistic" is and has been used to refer to a number of quite definite theses in jurisprudence.

Professor H. L. A. Hart has found that this usage applies to five propositions.[15] The first is that laws are the commands of a sovereign. As commands, laws are understood by the positivist as imperatives, not as descriptions of rules rooted in man's nature or as discoveries of an objective legal order. As commands of a

---

14 References to recent positivistic and analytic efforts to understand power are given in Chapter Nine.

15 See H. L. A. Hart, "Positivism and the Separation of Law and Morals," *Harvard Law Review*, 71 (1958), 601.

sovereign, laws are specifically related to observable features in the governmental system—the sovereign himself, the courts, or some other department. Second is the contention that there is no necessary connection between law and morals, or between law as it is and law as it ought to be. Third is the conviction that the analysis or study of meaning of legal concepts is worth pursuing, and is to be distinguished from other inquiries of a historical or sociological kind. This thesis has become even more important in the writings of recent positivists. Fourth is the belief that the legal order is a "closed logical system" in which correct legal decisions can be deduced from predetermined legal rules. Last is the philosophic assertion that moral judgments cannot be taken as statements of fact, or be established by rational argument or evidence. This theory is often referred to as the "emotive theory of value."

Of these five points, the second is perhaps the most distinctive of a positivistic philosophy of law.[16] What it does in effect is to make systems of value or conceptions of natural law irrelevant to jurisprudence. The task of jurisprudence is the elaboration and clarification of law as it actually exists in the modern state.

An early example of this approach is found in the work of John Chipman Gray (1839–1915).[17] The philosophy of law, Gray asserted, must start with the recognition of the truth that the law is not an ideal, but something that actually exists. "It is not that which is in accordance with religion, or nature, or morality, it is not that which it ought to be, but that which it is." On this basis, Gray defined the law itself as what judges lay down as rules of conduct: "the law consists of rules recognized and acted on by the courts of justice." These rules are given to protect and advance human interests, and they ascribe certain rights to persons, elaborating this protection. Thus rights are also determined by judges, who settle on the facts and who provide the rules according to which legal consequences may be deduced from the facts.

Perhaps the most influential legal positivist, however, is Hans Kelsen (1881–1973), who developed, as the title of his major work,

[16] The first is also important historically, for men like Machiavelli, Bodin, and Hobbes enunciated command theories of law, as did the utilitarian Austin. The so-called analytic jurisprudence owes something to all these men.

[17] *The Nature and Sources of Law*, New York, 1909.

Pure Theory of Law (Berkeley, 1967), suggests, a "pure" or scientific theory of law. Such a theory, he believed, must study the law as it is, not as the reflection of some moral ideal ("justice") that a people might hold. This he maintained by arguing that if law is to be viewed as a part of morals, an absolute moral value must be socially established. Moral absolutes, however, need to be rejected in a scientific point of view. Consequently, the legal order is independent of any moral order or value. To be sure, the legal system rests upon a pure legal norm, but this norm is entirely a procedural standard. Kelsen therefore concluded that the function of a theory of law is to produce a value-free description adequate to the kind of social reality law is.

PROBLEM V: POLITICAL OBLIGATION

Positivists and social scientists who follow their lead do not isolate the problem of political obligation as some other philosophers, with their more ethical bent, are inclined to do. This is because their assumptions rather direct them to social causes and influences and to the role of such causes in establishing social conformity. To put this observation somewhat paradoxically, the purported moral problem of obligation is transmuted into the scientific problem of control.

No more direct statement of such a position can be found than in the writings of the founder of sociology, Auguste Comte, to whom positivistic social theory, if not philosophy,[18] continues to be indebted. Many of Comte's ideas, such as his law of three stages and his social determinism, have been presented in preceding material. Comte also shared many ideas with Saint-Simon, whose follower he was for a time. His theory of obligation is developed within the context of these conceptions.

[18] Comte did not, as a matter of fact, have much influence on the philosophical movement of the early twentieth century known as logical positivism, even though the two shared some basic ideas. Logical positivism is discussed below in Chapter Nine.

Basically Comte's view is that as knowledge increases, the need for spiritual authority in society will be felt and met. That is, the progress of science will so affect men that the authority needed to assure the use of knowledge for their own good will rise among them. (It will be remembered that Comte and Saint-Simon believed that the influence of science is socially important more in relation to a changed vision of man and his place in the world than as a result of particular discoveries.) The recognition of this need is part of what Comte called positive morality.

Positive morality is of course to be based on Comte's positive philosophy. Through education and social control, good habits will be developed among the members of society that will establish the universal obligations of civilized men. Since education is also based on the positive philosophy, the obligations rooted in man's "social sentiment" will be most fully developed, for positivism alone adequately comprehends human nature. Among the consequences of this development, Comte inferred, will be the establishment of social subordination or hierarchy based on the same principles as biological classification. The highest level will be speculative (scientific and artistic) and the practical (industrial) classes; [19] other social classes will be ordered beneath them. When the gradation is established, it will be preserved from confusion by the consciousness that each order is subordinate to the grade above it as a condition of its superiority to those below it. A second consequence is that "the most important object of this regenerated polity will be the substitution of Duties for Rights." Since no supernatural claims are admissible in positivist society, the idea of right will in fact disappear—it is a "metaphysical" notion. Everyone will thus have duties, but rights in the ordinary sense will be claimed by no one.

Although Comte with the Saint-Simonians valued happiness more than freedom and insisted on a rule of a knowledgeable elite, he nevertheless felt that the spiritual power must be "popular." This it will be, he thought, through its impartial concern for the

---

[19] Comte's rather elaborate presentation of his "Religion of Humanity" with its priests and rituals, also part of this hierarchy, is an interesting, if eccentric, proposal. Hostile critics view it as nonsense; friendly critics find Comte attempting, even if inadequately, to find ways to satisfy man's emotional needs.

lower classes. The spiritual authority is obligated to secure education and employment for all members of society, just as they in
turn recognize their subordination to higher authority. Comte
thus answers the questions of the obligation of ruler to ruled and
of ruled to ruler in terms of the goal of human satisfactions made
possible by the universal application of scientific knowledge.

PROBLEM VI: THE IDEAL OF JUSTICE

It remains now to follow the implications of positivism for
the ideal of justice. Among the various themes of positivism that
have been surveyed in preceding sections is the conviction that
explanations of social phenomena and realities must be made
without recourse to transcendent or metaphysical notions. Values
are not unimportant to the positivist, but he insists that they be
understood within the context of human life. In society men
develop rules and standards to govern the concrete relations of
their lives, and their ideal conception of these relationships is their
conception of justice.

Discussions of justice often (and usefully) divide the concept
into two parts, formal and substantive. Now formal justice, as was
seen in the section on Law and Rights, is primarily a procedural
norm; and since the legal institutions of a society can be studied
scientifically and the meaning of procedural justice can be clarified
by such study, positivism can embrace this notion of justice. Its
precise meaning, though, can best be found in the work of judges
and lawyers.[20] Substantive justice, on the other hand, is frequently
viewed as a transcendent ideal. But given his rejection of transcendent principles and his emotive or nonobjectivist theory of
values, the positivist finds that he must understand substantive
justice within the orbit of sociological fact.

[20] Justice Holmes, while basically a pragmatist, reflected the statements of this
paragraph in his often quoted judgment that the law is a prophecy of what
the courts in fact will do. Holmes' views are touched on in Chapter Seven.

Heir of Comte and important contributor to sociological re-
search, Lucien Lévy-Bruhl (1857–1939) is a recent spokesman for
a positivistic view of justice. His position on justice may be
ⵏ⁻ divided into three parts.[21] First is his rejection of alternative views,
particularly of natural law theories of ethics and justice. Even if
these theories are presented in pseudoscientific form (as Lévy-Bruhl
believed some of them are), their fundamental falseness is apparent
in the light of an elementary knowledge of sociology. Sociological
data show that the formulas of justice come from the social realities existing at each epoch in the history of a society, and that
progress or change in ideals of justice is not attributable to some
conception of justice preexisting innately and universally in the
minds of men.

2- The second part of Lévy-Bruhl's position is his constructive
analysis of justice as a rule or ideal in society. The classical formulas
such as "giving every man his due" and "treating equals as equals"
are in themselves only empty statements. They receive their
signification and value from the social reality which imposes on
individuals the manner in which they should live. And this social
reality, Lévy-Bruhl believed, is not governed by a special series of
social phenomena like ethics or law. Rather, he posited a "law of
solidarity of the social series" which, among other things, refers to
the ways in which the various elements of a society such as its
＊ economic basis, its law, its beliefs, and its conscience intermingle
and affect one another. This law also refers to the effects of the
synthesis of reactions that the consciousness of an individual exercises upon other individuals. To remain stable, societies must relate,
and to some extent integrate, these elements and experiences in a
commonly held value system. Present in the value system are many
ideal conceptions, including justice as a legal norm, which relate
the members of societies in their respective duties and obligations
toward one another. Lévy-Bruhl in fact developed his positivistic
theory of value as a fundamental condition of social solidarity, for
it allowed him to view the various aspects of a society in their lived
interrelationships rather than as a priori elaborations of "foreign"
moral norms.

[21] See *Ethics and Moral Science,* trans. Elizabeth Lee, London, 1905.

ᵃ˙ The third part of Lévy-Bruhl's statement, which follows upon the preceding analysis, is his admonition to societies to follow the positivist endorsement of science. "To be truly rational, our action on social reality ought not to be guided by an abstract ideal . . . but by the results of science." Science will determine how the obligations of conscience are established, strengthened, and related to social life, and how they can be modified to produce progress.

Bibliographical Essay

Much of the literature covering early positivistic theories centers on Machiavelli, Hobbes, Saint-Simon, and Comte. Standard histories of philosophy are helpful, as are the following studies that provide a basic literature on the movement: J. S. Mill, *Auguste Comte and Positivism*, 5th ed., London, 1907; J. W. Allen, *Political Thought in the Sixteenth Century*, London, 1928; Herbert Butterfield, *The Statecraft of Machiavelli*, London, 1940; James Burnham, *The Machiavellians*, New York, 1943; Friedrich Meinecke, *Machiavellism: The Doctrine of Raison d'État and Its Place in Modern History*, New Haven, 1957; and two books by Leo Strauss, *The Political Philosophy of Hobbes*, Oxford, 1936, and Chicago, 1952, and *Thoughts on Machiavelli*, Glencoe, Ill., 1958. An important work in social philosophy by a contemporary positivist is Karl Popper's *The Open Society and Its Enemies*, Princeton, 1950, 4th ed., 1963; and B. F. Skinner's two works, *Walden II*, New York, 1948, and *Beyond Freedom and Dignity*, London, 1973, express the views of a psychologist who accepts the notion of scientific social engineering. Students may also find interesting the book by R. L. Hawkins on *Positivism in the United States*, Cambridge, Mass., 1938. Bibliographical materials on contemporary logical positivism are given below under analytic philosophy.

The "spirit of science" so central to positivist philosophy has also been uppermost in the methodology of much twentieth-century social science, including sociology, political science, psychology, and economics. Whole libraries of books have, of course, been produced in each of these fields, and mention of them is impossible here. Students of these disciplines who are alert to the meaning of positivism may find it important to examine the methodological and philosophical assumptions of the authors they are reading.

Philosophical Liberalism

Our third perspective in social philosophy involves a terminological problem. On the one hand, many of the themes and positions taken by its representatives are shared by thinkers of other philosophic schools. On the other hand, while there is a common core of ideas about society and government among them, there is also a rather wide divergence of views in other areas such as religion and metaphysics. Creating even further difficulty is the fact that while there is good historical ground for using the term liberalism regarding this group—many historians have said that John Locke's views are the very soul of liberalism—there are also good reasons for using the same term when referring to many utilitarians in the nineteenth century and to certain socialist positions in the twentieth century. In actual practice, liberalism seems to be used to denote positions covering a range from those centering on the interests of the middle class to the culmination of the whole Western political tradition. One could perhaps speak of a classical liberalism, although it may confuse this perspective with anticipations of liberalism in Greek and Roman thought; or perhaps of Enlightenment liberalism, although this might suggest that all Enlightenment social philosophers were liberals, which would be misleading also. Thus, it seems necessary to be somewhat arbitrary in the matter of names. Liberalism will be used in this book to refer to a scheme of ideas in social philosophy that, historically, did arise during the time of the Enlightenment (though many of its conceptions have been influential to the present day) and that presents a distinctive perspective in social philosophy. So understood, philosophical liberalism must be sharply distinguished from political liberalism which, as a political position, may derive from many philosophical roots.

More important than the matter of names, however, are the chief ideas of the liberal position. Perhaps the best starting point in discussing them is the liberal's belief that there are moral rules that men ought to obey simply because they are men. Unlike Hobbes, for example, the liberal asserts that men are by nature moral beings and that although society does enter into the development of human nature, there are rules men ought to obey because they have certain given capacities. As Locke put it, the "keeping of faith belongs to men as men and not as members of society."

The recognition of man as a moral being may suggest that the liberal is returning to some of the themes of classical realism. While the early liberals were influenced by medieval thought, their chief inspiration came from the ancient school of Stoicism. In fact, one of the defining characteristics of philosophical liberalism is its acceptance of Stoic values and of a number of ideas associated with them.

Flourishing from the third century B.C. to the fifth century A.D., Stoicism was primarily an ethical doctrine. Moral life was understood in terms of control of the emotions and passions by reason. Human beings, as the Stoics saw them, constantly experience unhappiness and misery for lack of this control; they become emotionally involved with things and persons to such a degree that these objects cannot support the involvement. An example or two from Epictetus (60–110), one of the greatest Stoics, may explain this point. "If you are fond of a jug," he wrote, "say you are fond of a jug; then you will not be disturbed if it is broken. If you kiss your child or your wife, say to yourself that you are kissing a human being, for then if death strikes it, you will not be disturbed."

The Stoic offered two maxims of advice in order to prevent this disturbance. He said that men should live "according to nature"; through their rational powers they should recognize and understand the natures of things—jugs and human beings—and the laws that govern them. An earthen thing must not be confused with a living being, nor a finite being confused with an infinite one. Secondly, the Stoic said that men should live in "inde-

✳ pendence of externals." Some matters lie within man's power, others do not. In man's power is his will; and so he is free to act or not to act, to get or to avoid. Not in man's power, however, are the natures of things and the laws that govern them.[1] Thus not only right reason but right will or virtue was involved in the Stoic's search for the good life. The Stoic sage who achieved this goal experienced the tranquility and freedom that are the marks of a completed and fulfilled human life.

Stoicism also developed a rather complete metaphysical context for its ethical teachings. Since the universe acts in accordance with causal laws, it may be considered rational; and since it is rational, it is also divine. But men are also rational beings, and they therefore share in the divinity of the universe. Reason is a spark of the divine in men, and is the basis of individual rights and dignity. And, since all men are rational beings, they are and must be treated as equals. Unlike many of their contemporaries, Stoics held that even those who are slaves under positive law are equal to free men and have rights before the law of nature. The equality of men implies the brotherhood of men, and the universal law of the universe making men brothers means that men are citizens of the cosmos—cosmopolitans—before they are Greek or Roman.

Through these ideas, Stoicism exerted an extensive influence on political theory. It produced a new moral sanction for politics outside the Greek polis, and it taught the doctrine of a pervading natural law, rooted in the order of nature and moral in content. Its emphasis was on the individual and his rights, and it based its appeal and sanction on reason. Most fundamental of all was its postulate that values inhere ultimately in the satisfactions and realizations of personality.

As philosophical liberalism developed in the seventeenth and eighteenth centuries, it accepted this inheritance from Stoicism and built upon it. Like Stoicism, liberalism sought to produce new moral sanctions for politics outside the medieval world and in the face of what it took to be the nonmoralism of positivism. It too appealed to natural law to answer questions of obligation, rights,

[1] Stoic metaphysics was in fact deterministic: all things in nature happen by causal necessity..

and morality; it stressed individualism and individual rights; it sought to justify its position by an appeal to reason. To this cluster of ideas, however, must be added two further conceptions, namely limited government and the centrality of freedom. Liberalism in all its forms is marked by a distrust of government; power and authority must be limited by the ends they serve, for they are but means to an end. They are to be judged by reference to their purpose as well as by the regularities of the natural law that define mutual obligations and duties.

Philosophical liberals have generally adhered to some form of democratic government as being best suited to their convictions that coercion is justified, not for national greatness, nor to enable men to attain virtue, nor for the sake of heaven, nor in the service of a common good transcending individual rights, but only because government is needed to secure the proper ends for individuals. That proper end, as liberals see it, is freedom. This political ideal is of course common to many philosophies; but liberalism gives it both a central importance and an individualistic meaning. Freedom is each man's right to live as seems good to him, provided he respects the same right in others. From this understanding of freedom come the correlative ideals of toleration and freedom of conscience, which are the special marks of the liberal's concern with freedom.

The philosophic judgments of liberalism thus involve an acceptance of Stoic values, especially individualism, moralism, and reason, a recommendation that government be limited in scope and authority, and a postulation of the ideal of freedom as the consummate political value. Having many spokesmen of its principles, liberalism developed into and remains one of the major alternatives in Western political philosophy.

PROBLEM I: MAN AND SOCIETY

Unlike the Hobbesian, positivistic assertion that morality is consequent upon and derived from society, the philosophical liberal is convinced that man is by nature a moral being. Society may enter into and form man's conscience, and it may even be taken as a necessary condition for any realization of man's capacities for moral behavior, but fundamental to liberalism are the two convictions that man is naturally a moral agent and that there are independent rules or laws that man must follow to realize himself as such an agent. As John Locke said, "Obligations cease not in the state of nature."

The expression state of nature is common (though not universal) in the writings of liberals. Among the many uses to which it is put [2] is that of understanding man's moral capacities. In the state of nature—that is, apart from society (the state of nature need not be considered a historical state at all, though it was by some liberals)—men are reasonable and moral, active in the pursuit of certain values, and guided by rational moral norms. In that state they also are, to some extent, weak and defenseless; the need for association in society under government arises from this weakness.

The details of such a position were given their first philosophically important statement by John Locke (1632–1704), who was led to many of his assertions about man and society by his reflections on the problem of knowledge.[3] As an empiricist, Locke took the basic elements of knowledge to be simple sensory experiences—his own list included yellow, white, heat, cold, soft, hard, bitter, sweet. When these simple ideas are compounded, they produce complex ideas, and when complex ideas are taken to represent particular existing things, they are ideas of substances. To put this theory another way: it is the combination of qualities such as color, odor, and shape that results in the idea of a thing. Since these qualities cannot be believed to be floating about with no binding principle that accounts for their togetherness, a sub-

---

[2] Discussion here is limited to the meaning of the state of nature in relation to man's moral nature and the origins of society; later sections touch upon other problems such as government, law, and obligation, where the concept is also important.

[3] See especially Locke's *Two Treatises on Government, Letter on Toleration,* and *An Essay Concerning Human Understanding,* all of which are widely available in paperback editions.

stance is postulated as their substratum. This substratum fulfills the need of providing unity of qualities, even though the real essence of substance is unknowable.

The idea of a mental or spiritual substance arises in much the same way. Corresponding to the qualities that result in the idea of a thing are experiences such as doubting, fearing, and feeling. These too cannot exist "unattached" or of themselves, and hence an immaterial mental substratum must exist to support them.

> *By supposing a substance wherein thinking, knowing, doubting, and a power of moving, etc. do subsist, we have as clear a notion of the substance of spirit, as we have of body, the one being supposed to be (without knowing what it is) the substratum of those simple ideas we have from without, and the other supposed (with a like ignorance of what it is) to be the substratum to those operations we experiment in ourselves within.*

Thus, Locke's theory of knowledge was the basis of his understanding of man as mental substance. It meant, as Locke inferred, that there is a new view of the state of nature and a new content for the "law of reason." A person is mental substance: one's rights, even one's own body, are now his "property." Religion is concerned properly only with this substance: hence toleration, not theocracy; democracy, not divine right. There is no natural relation among these substances (as, for example, the natural spatial relation among physical substances), hence "hierarchies" or political aristocracies are neither natural nor in the nature of things. No authority can grasp the essentially unknowable mental substance; hence men must submit to authority only as they agree to do so, and in all cases each man is the best judge of himself. All social relations are conventions, including the relation of law, and conventions have authority solely through the consent of the related.

On the basis of this view of man, Locke stated in his social philosophy that in the state of nature men are equally and perfectly free to order themselves and their possessions as they think fit. This freedom and equality are governed by a law of nature that obliges everyone to respect the freedom of self-determination in others, binding persons by the natural law to treat others as equals. In addition to refraining from interference with the rights of others, men in the state of nature have the right to punish transgressors of their rights "as calm reason and conscience dictate." The law of nature is thus a law of freedom. It is supported not by custom or tradition but by reason, which defines the rights and duties that constitute and sustain freedom.

Yet men find it necessary to give up their natural freedom and form a society. This they do because they find that the enjoyment of their natural rights in the state of nature is uncertain. The state of nature lacks (1) a settled, known law, (2) impartial judges, and (3) the power to enforce decisions and prevent infractions. Hence, men are driven to enter into a "social contract" where they give up their power of punishing transgressors and of doing whatever they think fit for their preservation in exchange for the collective and stronger action of society and government.[4] Through the social compact men agree to live in the bonds of civil society. The compact creates one body that acts by the consent of the majority, and by agreeing to the compact, individuals place themselves under the obligation to submit to the determinations of the majority.

Thus the existence of society and the authority of government arise for Locke out of men's freely given consent,[5] not out of their needs. To be sure, men need society and government, but it does not follow that because they need society, they cannot take care of themselves. The "one body" that men create is a device of human wisdom to meet their needs as rational and moral beings; since they are the only adequate judges of their needs, they take care of themselves by establishing a civil society. The authority men so establish is strictly derivative from their act, and the power of the commonwealth is a trust, limited by the ends it serves and the judgments citizens make of it. The end of the commonwealth is to secure and preserve property—"life, liberty, and estate"—or, since property for Locke is synonymous with individual rights,[6] the

---

[4] Whether the compact is social or governmental is unclear in Locke. Althusius and Pufendorf made it clearer by proposing two contracts, one for society, a second for government.

[5] This key doctrine is explored in the section on "Political Obligation."

[6] Generally, that is. Locke does occasionally speak of property in the restricted sense, thus becoming at times a spokesman of Whiggism.

end of civil society may be said to be the preservation of freedom. In matters pertaining to rights, but in none other, government must use force.

Natural rights and law, moralism, individualism, society as derivative, and government as limited are the themes of the liberal's understanding of man and society. The thought of Locke is their *locus classicus*. However much of Locke's own philosophical framework has been rejected by other and later liberals (and few philosophers today would stand on, for example, Locke's epistemology), the social theory he enunciated remains a major philosophical alternative.

Problem II: Social and Political Values

Little mention can be made of any aspect of philosophical liberalism without touching on its values and ideals, for a kind of moralism pervades its answers to basic social and political questions. It is important, nevertheless, to bring these values forward for explicit treatment. In addition to Locke, whose thought we have just surveyed, the writings of Montesquieu (1689–1755) give early expression to liberal values.

Montesquieu's major work, *The Spirit of the Laws*, is a wide-ranging and diffuse book that occasionally states doctrines that are difficult to classify. As the title indicates, the study seeks to uncover the *spirit* of laws, an effort that took Montesquieu into many aspects of history as well as into the gradually expanding, yet still infant, science of comparative anthropology. The relative simplicity of the available data allowed Montesquieu to make generalizations and classifications that a more recent writer would be embarrassed to develop. Yet his penetrating insights and superior style save the work from oblivion and indeed make it still valuable to the student today.

The spirit of the laws of a society depends on many factors— environment, forms of government, values held by citizens—and

Montesquieu explored them all in the light of the evidence he had. While his method seems factual and empirical, he nevertheless had his own preferences and values, and he was not adverse to expressing them or judging situations by them. As with Locke and other philosophical liberals, Montesquieu's chief concern was with freedom and equality. Liberty, he said, "can consist only in doing what we ought to will, and in not being constrained to do what we ought not to do." This may seem to be a more authoritarian definition than Locke's "right to live as seems good to the individual" until it is remembered that Montesquieu gave his definition an individualistic setting. For liberals generally, liberty is not a matter of being consistent with the common good as in realism; nor as with Hobbes, the right to do what the laws do not forbid; nor as in Machiavelli, the right to participate in government; nor as with Bodin, the security of external possessions and family rights: liberty is essentially the right of self-determination limited only by respect for the same right of others.

Montesquieu found that *virtue* is the essential principle of democracies, but the "natural place of virtue is near to liberty." With other liberals, he was interested in equality as a condition of freedom (though he also asserted that when the spirit of equality is either extinct or extreme, the principle of democracy is corrupt) and in the structure of governmental organization as a preserver of freedom. The latter problem of Montesquieu and other liberals is treated in the next section.

· A second document expressing liberal values and having a continuing influence in the contemporary world is the Declaration of Independence. This historically important state paper is an almost perfect brief summary of the fundamental assumptions of philosophical liberalism as the American Enlightenment sought to express them. Confidence in the beneficent order of Nature, as Montesquieu would put it, is manifest in the appeal of the first paragraph to "the separate and equal station to which the Laws of Nature and of Nature's God entitle them." The criterion used in the second paragraph is self-evidence, a rationalistic, almost mathematical principle. This itself is significant, for by its use of self-evidence, the Declaration is rejecting many of the traditional sanctions of political values such as metaphysics and theology. Men are created equal or, as Locke wrote, "Princes indeed are born superior unto other men in power, but in nature equal." Men are as well endowed with "certain inalienable Rights," and they institute governments to secure them. Perhaps the most important word in the entire document is "deriving," for the just powers of government derive from the consent of the governed. Government is an agency serving human rights, and "whenever any Form of Government becomes destructive of these ends, it is the Right of the People to alter or to abolish it, and to institute new Government." The remainder of the Declaration presents detailed charges against invasions by the British crown on the rights of people.

These ideals and principles—equality, rights, life, liberty, estate, happiness, consent—are to be counted among the traditional liberal values. They are also matters of reason, for the liberals of the day drew the implication from Sir Isaac Newton's work that the method of reason should be used to reach secure conclusions in moral and political affairs. Regularities and certainties are available to open eyes and inquiring minds; and the values that should govern the affairs of men are among those certainties.

PROBLEM III: STATE, POWER, AND AUTHORITY

For philosophical liberals, the state with its power and authority is just and legitimate when it is organized for freedom, and a number of distinctive doctrines have been stated by liberals in developing this insight. The first is the theory of the social compact, which suggests that just government is established by individuals who, through an act of association, consent to a common authority as the agent of their rights.[7] The people are sovereign,

---

[7] The compact need not be thought of as an historical act: its point is ethical, since it is concerned with the nature of just government. It may be noted that the notion of a social contract is much older than liberalism, having been formulated by Lycophron in classical Greece.

authority is derived from and sanctioned by them, and—resting as it does on consent [8]—the compact is limited and conditional.

So common and basic to philosophical liberalism is the theory of the social contract that almost all the sections of this chapter include references to it. One influential statement of the theory not yet mentioned, however, is found in the writings of Jean Jacques Rousseau (1712–1778), especially his *Contrat Social*. Rousseau is a complex figure who is exceedingly difficult to classify firmly, for many strands run through his thought and not always consistently. Writing at the end of the Enlightenment and at the beginning of Romanticism, he reflected both movements. He praised the life of feeling, even to disparage reason, yet he believed that justice, for example, is a norm of reason. He seemed at times to find Locke and other liberals too individualistic, yet he believed that individuals have rights, and he defined sovereignty to include these rights. His theory sets up a notion of a general will that has been interpreted as a forerunner of totalitarian states and that paradoxically can force individuals to be free, but he also firmly asserted that justice can never be denied an individual on the pretext that government is serving the common good. Small wonder that there are different interpretations of Rousseau! Nevertheless, there are good grounds for including him in the liberal perspective, primarily for his love of freedom and of equality as a means to freedom.

Rousseau's problem is to explain how a just society can arise. He was convinced that the existing societies of his day were corrupt and enslaving: they made men dependent rather than free and— Stoic values lie behind this judgment—gave them false desires. He was also convinced that men are naturally good, and that the good society would be one that conformed to man's nature and to the freedom that is man's birthright. The problem of political subjection is thus primarily ethical and only secondarily a matter of law and power. Rousseau found its solution in the social compact, which is an act where each person, in giving himself to all, gives himself to no one. A moral and collective body is established that

[8] See Problem V for further treatment of this notion.

is itself controlled by the "general will." [9] By this somewhat difficult notion Rousseau meant not simply the will of all or of the majority, but the will to justice, to impartiality, to the treatment of the good of others as equally important with one's own good.

The compact thus explains political organization as the product of a personal act of each citizen. It establishes a moral authority dedicated to justice and it aims at freedom, for freedom is obedience to laws men prescribe to themselves. It maintains the consent of the governed and the sovereignty of the people, a sovereignty that is indivisible and inalienable. In all these particulars, Rousseau's theory is precisely the democracy liberals came to understand.

The second major doctrine of philosophical liberals is really a collection of ideas about the structure of government. The notions of derived authority and limited government are implicit in liberal values, and many liberal philosophers wrote about the structure that government should have to reflect liberal values. Montesquieu, with whom the principle of the separation of powers is especially associated, was an eloquent spokesman of the idea that power must be circumscribed in appropriate ways if freedom is to be preserved. Power, he thought, must be limited by power, and the basic branches of government check the possible abuses of each other. The separation of the judiciary prevents oppression in contempt of the law, and the separation of the legislative and executive branches prevents oppressions by means of the law. Closely related to the system of checks and balances is the principle of federalism, which holds that different levels of government—local, regional, and national—must have separate and distinct exercises. And finally, liberals have also written of representative

---

[9] While much in Rousseau's theory up to this point resembles Locke's views, the introduction of this notion by Rousseau initiated a series of philosophic moves that led to basic differences between the two men—and to highly differing evaluations of Rousseau's work as well. One commentator, George H. Sabine, has suggested that Locke's liberal position stresses liberty and pluralism as basic values, while Rousseau took equality as the primary social value. See Sabine's article, "The Two Concepts of Democracy," *The Philosophic Review*, 61 (1953), 451–74. Interested readers should consult not only this study but Locke's and Rousseau's own writings as well.

government as a scheme to maintain the people's control over the agency dealing with their interests.

PROBLEM IV: LAW AND RIGHTS

Natural rights and natural law have already emerged in preceding discussions of liberalism, and they are indeed central concepts for the position. Like many political ideas, however, they have had a long history. Plato and Aristotle mention natural laws, the Stoics held firmly to a law based on the nature of things, and Aquinas, as we have seen, made the natural law one of the main features of his philosophy of law. On the whole, liberalism is in this same tradition, differing from it not so much in the content as in the method of establishing and knowing the natural law.

Natural law may be defined as the expression, in the form of law, of an order of right relations essential to man that he is obliged to realize and obey. The function of the doctrine is to posit an objective moral principle for the right ordering of man and society. Thus understood, the definition applies generally to natural law positions, including realism. Philosophical liberals, however, develop the theory further with particular reference to their individualism and their rationalism. Positing a state of nature and the derivative status of authority, liberals see the natural law as an order necessary for individual development and happiness, and natural rights as specifications of the conditions for developing human capacities that a right order would respect. Although Locke's influential theory of man as mental substance has been stated earlier, it should be further noted that the "nature" of man upon which the natural law rests is not so much an empirical datum as an obligation (this is why the nature of man is expressed in the form of a duty or a law). Man is a datum in experience through his capabilities such as reason and freedom; his function is to develop and exercise these capabilities in conformity with the law of his nature.

Individualistic in emphasis, the liberals' doctrine of natural law is also rationalistic. It substitutes the authority of reason for the spiritual authority of divine law and for the positivists' authority of force. Moral ideas, liberals traditionally have held, are based on relations of congruity (in this regard, they are like mathematics); they are formed by the mind, and can conform to the objective order prescribed by the "Divine Legislator." Even further, moral ideas can be demonstrated, for they have relations of "connection and agreement" (Locke) that can be discovered by the inspection of the mind. By deduction, therefore, men can possess moral and political truth in a "self-evident" way, as the Declaration of Independence puts it. Although twentieth-century philosophical liberalism does not always accept all of these inherited ideas, as will be seen in Problem VI, the ideal of rationality they imply for social affairs remains.

One other important historical development in liberal philosophy of law remains to be mentioned. By their establishment of a theory of government and law through reason, the early liberals were the founders of an independent and purely rationalistic system of natural law and natural right. The first legal theorist to move toward such a system was Hugo Grotius (1583–1645), especially in his major work on the rights of war and peace.[10] Here he sought to prove that a "law of nations" governing the relations of sovereign states exists and is rooted not in positive law but in natural law. Within the context of this aim, Grotius defined a right as a moral quality annexed to a person and a natural right as a dictate of right reason. Natural rights indicate things that are binding or unlawful in themselves; like the mathematical relation that twice two is four, natural rights refer to an objective order that is eternally and universally valid and that cannot be changed even by God himself. Also like mathematical relations, the order of natural rights involves moral regularities that are available to and can be known by any reasonable mind. Natural rights and law thus constitute an autonomous domain, for their validity is independent of positions or conclusions held in metaphysics or religion. Grotius was

[10] *The Rights of War and Peace*, trans. A. C. Campbell, Washington, 1901.

thus one of the first to cut the cord of dependence of legal theory and to attempt to make it a separate science.

Problem V: Political Obligation

Among the many doctrines of philosophical liberalism, none is more fundamental than the theory of nature and limits of political obligation. Questions as to what makes a government legitimate, why citizens are obliged to obey laws, and whether governments ought to respect limits of their authority are all involved. The chief notion by which these questions are answered, namely the consent of the governed, has been mentioned and utilized in discussions of many of the topics in preceding sections. Both the state of nature and the social compact, however artificial they may seem, are intimately connected with the idea of a limited government based on the consent of its citizens.

John Locke, the major philosophic spokesman of this idea, used it to answer what for him was the central political question, namely the legitimacy of government. Consent, he argued, is the only possible basis of just subjection to authority. To be sure, Locke found it necessary to use "consent" in a variety of ways—sometimes he meant voluntary agreement, at other times a personal and deliberate act of choice. He also had to distinguish between express and tacit consent. The former, occurring when one takes up citizenship in a country, for example, is clear enough. Tacit consent to a government is merely implicit, but it is given, Locke believed, simply if a man has possessions located within the territory of a society, or if a person resides within or passes through that territory. His argument for this is that the act of assent to the social compact places all property under the regulation of government, and therefore to possess property is to agree to that regulation. Difficult as some aspects of this doctrine of tacit consent may be, the principle that Locke was seeking to uphold by it is that every obligation must be laid on oneself voluntarily. Governments are thus legitimate when they rest on consent.

Though Locke was not interested in developing a theory of government in all its details, and did not do so, there is one proposition that he did specify as following from the idea of consent. This is the supremacy of the legislative function of government, which is given by the people and which is sacred and unalterable when so given. All obligation, he wrote, terminates in this supreme power. Thus, the question of why citizens are obliged to obey government is answered again by Locke: it is because government is basically their own act and preference.

But does government have obligations to its citizens that constitute limits for it? Locke answered with an emphatic yes. The authority of government is limited by the nature of the end it serves—the preservation of life, liberty, and estate. When government does this, it may use force, and the obligation to obey is direct and complete. Government may not use force in other matters such as religion, for it has not been entrusted to concern itself with them. If the state should transgress beyond its limits, a trust is broken, the contract becomes void, and the people may institute a new agency for their rights.

In his writings Locke specified some of the ways that government must act to be true to its proper end as, for example, rule by known laws. These too follow from Locke's conception of the purpose of government. But his fundamental assumptions about contract and consent are the heart of his and the liberal position. People are obliged to obey government as the agent and protector of their rights, and government is obliged to serve its citizens because its very existence is derivative from them. Government and rights are two sides of the same coin, held together by the doctrine of consent.

PROBLEM VI: THE IDEAL OF JUSTICE

The methodological and philosophical grounds of traditional liberalism's views of rights, law, and justice have been outlined above. Placing its trust in an objective moral order and in the power of reason to apprehend it, philosophical liberalism understands justice as that rational order where the law of nature is obeyed and the nature of man realized. The natural law, justice, and reason are nearly synonymous, and all three have an objective, universal meaning for the liberal.

Unlike Hobbes, the liberal denies that consent and compact bring justice into being; rather, the compact is founded on justice. Unlike utilitarianism, to which we shall come next in our study, liberalism denies that justice and freedom are externally related merely as means to end, and accordingly, the latter theory asserts that justice is the order of freedom or the realization of freedom itself. As a good and rational order, justice is that structure in which individuals are protected and encouraged in their right to the things of this world—life, liberty, and estate.

The most influential contemporary statement of a liberal theory of justice, and of a liberal view of society as well, is found in the masterpiece by John Rawls (1921–   ), *A Theory of Justice* (1971).[11] Much of the older conceptual apparatus of philosophical liberalism is, of course, modernized; but Rawls retains for his treatment of justice such basic and defining notions as social contract, individualism, rights, and rationality. The theory he develops is called, after the title of one of his earlier articles, justice as fairness.

Basic to Rawls' contractarianism is his shift from viewing the social contract as an act to defining it in terms of procedure. The problem of justice, that is, is one of developing just procedures for determining what is fair or just; what obtains from following them will then itself be just. Since the problem of justice arises from the conflict of claims and rights among persons, Rawls' basic question about justice may be put more fully as follows: by what procedure can self-interested persons with legitimate competing claims adopt principles to insure just practices and institutions in their society?

[11] While Rawls' theory of justice is usually classified as liberal, there are actually many philosophical elements in it. Of particular importance is the influence of Immanuel Kant (see Chapter Five). The recognition of this influence is a reminder of the fact that philosophical liberalism is a collection of ideas centering on social individualism, and that it therefore frequently embraces additional philosophical concepts as well.

In setting about to answer his question, Rawls makes a number of assumptions about the "contract process" in which he hopes to find the meaning of justice. Chief of these assumptions are: (1) that human cooperation is possible and necessary, (2) that persons will on the whole adhere to principles of rational choice, (3) that persons desire primary goods such as liberty, opportunity, and income, (4) that the contract process is constrained by a minimum morality, and (5) that the parties to the contract are capable of a sense of justice.

The social contract is then interpreted as a hypothetical "original position" in which the parties to the contract are to choose the principles that will secure justice for their acts and social institutions. To insure impartiality in their choice, Rawls imagines them choosing behind the "veil of ignorance," which keeps each individual from knowing his talent, social class, the historical time of his society—indeed, from knowing anything about the unique circumstances of his life. From such an original position of choice, the contract process issues in two basic principles of justice. First, each person is to have an equal right to the most extensive total system of basic liberties compatible with a system of liberty for all; second, social and economic inequalities are to be arranged so that they are both (a) to the greatest benefit of the least advantaged, and (b) attached to offices and positions open to all under conditions of fair equality of opportunity. These principles define the content of substantive (not just formal) justice, and they are justified for Rawls because they emerge from a fair procedure of rational choice.

Bibliographical Essay

Liberal thought in the sense defined in this book has been given extensive treatment by historians and philosophers. Nearly all the volumes mentioned in the bibliography of the introductory chapter above contain chapters on that movement, as well as further bibliographical materials. Among the basic studies of liberalism is the following sample: G. P. Gooch, *The History of English*

Democratic Ideas in the Seventeenth Century, New York, 1912; T. H. Green, *Four Lectures on the English Revolution*, which is reprinted from his *Works*; and Kingsley Martin, *French Liberal Thought in the Eighteenth Century*, 2d ed., London, 1954. Liberalism in America is treated in such works as C. E. Merriam, *A History of American Political Theories*, New York, 1928; Louis Hartz, *The Liberal Tradition in America*, New York, 1955; and Robert N. Beck, *The Meaning of Americanism*, New York, 1956. Many philosophic studies of each of the figures discussed in this chapter can easily be found in institutional libraries. Though showing somewhat different emphases, the following books give philosophical expression to aspects of liberalism: M. R. Cohen, *Faith of a Liberal*, New York, 1946; L. T. Hobhouse, *The Metaphysical Theory of the State*, London, 1918; F. A. Hayek, *The Constitution of Liberty*, Chicago, 1960; as well as the writings of Herbert Spencer, who wrote of liberalism in a Darwinian as well as a modified Lockeian perspective. Anarchist thought is anthologized in L. I. Krimerman and Lewis Perry, *Patterns of Anarchy*, Garden City, 1966. Not all titles mentioning "liberalism" will be appropriate to this chapter, however; as the introduction suggested, the philosophical liberalism discussed here must be distinguished from the broader use of the term liberalism in political theory.

Utilitarianism

Utilitarians expound the theory that moral and political decisions are justified by their utility, that is, by their conduciveness to "the greatest good of the greatest number." The movement is largely English and, in the opinion of some writers, it is the most important contribution of English thought to ethics. (Utilitarian schools also flourished in France and, to a lesser extent, in America.) Founded by Richard Cumberland in his book, *De legibus naturae* (1672), utilitarianism reached full expression in David Hume's *A Treatise of Human Nature* (1739). Afterwards, the writings of the Benthamites dominated utilitarian thought, beginning with Jeremy Bentham's *A Fragment on Government* (1776) and *An Introduction to the Principles of Morals and Legislation* (1789), and ending with James Mill's *A Fragment on Mackintosh* (1835). Its most influential expression is given in John Stuart Mill's *Utilitarianism* (1861), and its most completely developed statement is in Henry Sidgwick's *Methods of Ethics* (1874).

"I am an adherent of the *Principle of Utility*," wrote Bentham,

> when I measure my approval or disapproval of any act, public or private, by its tendency to produce pains and pleasures; when I use the terms just, unjust, moral, immoral, good, bad, *as comprehensive terms which embrace the idea of certain pains and certain pleasures, and have no other meaning whatsoever.*

This quotation gives the general features of utilitarian moral theories. First, utilitarianism is hedonistic (from the Greek *hedone*, pleasure). Good means pleasure, evil means pain, and thus the greatest good and happiness mean the sum total of pleasures. Secondly, utilitarians teach directly and simply that of the various possibilities open to men, they ought to choose that which will produce the greatest happiness (pleasure) for the greatest number of persons. The determination of moral acts is made in terms of the consequences they produce. In ethical terminology, utilitarianism is a *teleological* ethics because of this emphasis on consequences and because the idea of "right" is defined and understood through relation to the good: what is right is what produces good.[1] Teleological ethical theories stand opposed to *deontological* theories that hold men ought to do what is inherently right as determined by a direct consideration of actions or by reference to some general formal principle.[2] Bentham suggested that other moral terms like just have no meaning except in relation to pleasure and pain.

What sort of proof do utilitarians offer for this assertion as well as for the principle of utility itself? Bentham stated[3] that utilitarianism is "self-referentially" true, for "when a man attempts to combat the principles of utility, it is with reasons drawn, without his being aware of it, from that very principle itself." Different in emphasis, though not completely dissimilar, is John Stuart Mill's discussion "Of What Sort of Proof the Principle of Utility Is Susceptible."[4] The only proof that an object is visible, he wrote, is that people actually see it. And in like manner, the sole evidence that anything is desirable is that people do actually desire it. "No reason can be given why the general happiness is desirable except that each person, so far as he believes it to be attainable, desires his own happiness."

[1] A modern refinement of utilitarianism distinguishes *act* and *rule* utility. This distinction is introduced below, Problem VI.

[2] Most historical theories of ethics actually contain both teleological and deontological elements; "pure" views are rare. In terms of theories thus far covered, utilitarianism is closest to a teleological theory, and the appeal to self-evidence in the Declaration of Independence mentioned above approximates a deontological theory.

[3] *An Introduction to the Principles of Morals and Legislation*, Chapter 1.

[4] Chapter 4 of *Utilitarianism*.

Finally, the quotation from Bentham, reflecting the antimetaphysical import of utilitarianism, suggests that apart from pleasure and pain, moral terms "have no other meaning whatsoever." As he also put it elsewhere, "Take away pleasures and pains [and] not only happiness, but justice and duty and obligation . . . are so many empty words." There are to be no metaphysical notions or "fictions" in ethics—pleasure and pain have empirical reference. There are objective standards, for ethical and political decisions are justified by their conduciveness to the greatest happiness for the greatest number. Utilitarianism thus proposes to build a system that will stand without the scaffolding of such ideas as natural law and right reason. As a philosophic movement, it reflects the expansion of scientific knowledge and philosophical criticism, which for many thinkers led to a fading of the authority of transcendent notions embodied in abstract reason.

The philosophic criticism alluded to is primarily that of David Hume (1711–1776), who was himself one of the great utilitarians.[5] Hume's discussion of knowledge and reason has affected the whole course of political philosophy. He subjected the concept of reason used by natural law theorists to careful analysis, and found it to involve a confusion of four ideas. The first is that any mere comparison of ideas is not related to fact. It is necessary to distinguish between mathematical certainty and empirical probability, between "relations of ideas" and "matters of fact." Relations of ideas such as logical and mathematical truths do give certainty, but Hume argued that they never can give men knowledge of fact. One way he tried to show this is by pointing out that the contradictory of any matter of fact is always possible—it is possible that the sun will not rise tomorrow, however hard it may be to believe—although the contradictory of a logical truth is always impossible. Perhaps his most famous use of this distinction relates to the analysis of causality. Cause and effect are two distinct events, and reasoning about them will not reveal any intrinsic causal relation between them. Only experience provides a basis for linking causes and effects. Further, if reason attempts to become "metaphysical" about causality, it falls into a logical circle. As Hume put it,

[5] See Hume's A *Treatise of Human Nature*, An *Enquiry concerning Human Understanding*, and An *Enquiry concerning the Principles of Morals*.

> *We have said that all arguments concerning existence are founded*
> *on the relation of cause and effect; that our knowledge of that*
> *relation is derived entirely from experience; and that all our ex-*
> *perimental conclusions proceed upon the supposition, that the*
> *future will be conformable to the past. To endeavor, therefore,*
> *the proof of this last supposition by probable arguments, or argu-*
> *ments regarding existence, must be evidently going in a circle,*
> *and taking that for granted which is the very point in question.*

The second idea about which natural law theories are confused concerns knowledge based on experience, according to Hume. Such knowledge yields only probability of judgment, not certainty, and the probabilities achieved by knowledge are limited to experience. Consequently, reason has no valid transcendent use and meta-physical skepticism is the result. Next, Hume argued that reason does not dictate to men a way of acting; if anything is good, it is so by reference to their desires, inclinations, and approvals. Reason is morally neutral and merely "obeys the passions." It is good enough to give direction and planning for obvious ends and thus to be an instrument of limited practical control, but it is powerless to discern ultimate ends or to motivate men toward them. Last is the distinction between *is* and *ought* statements. The former refer to facts, the latter to judgments about values and ideals, and Hume asserted that no value judgment can be inferred from premises that are wholly factual. Reason cannot derive an *ought* from an *is*, and if an *ought* is given in a conclusion, it is there either circularly (because it is also in a premise) or invalidly. The conclusion of a valid argument can contain nothing that is not contained in the premises.

In relation to many traditional philosophies, Hume's critique of reason is negative and destructive.[6] Yet, for the most part, its implications were accepted by utilitarians, and his philosophy marks a turning point in philosophical theory. Reason no longer reflects absolute values; hence political thought must be inter-preted in relative and human terms, with no religious or meta-

---

[6] Hume's work also influenced later positivism and much twentieth-century thought. There are many points of similarity between positivistic and utilitarian epistemologies; differences between them are mainly in ethical theory.

physical explanation behind it. Morality is not founded on the "dictates of right reason," for reason dictates no values. The basis and authority of value judgments, individual and social, must be referred to their utility and ultimately to human motives and human propensities to action.

Problem I: Man and Society

Utilitarians accept the main conclusions of Hume's destructive critique of reason. These conclusions imply that a rational basis for society, including natural law and rationalist ethics, is destroyed and that another foundation is required in its place. Utilitarians attempt to build this foundation by using a new account of human nature and moral experience and by the principle of utility. Again, David Hume provided a crucially significant doctrine of human nature for the utilitarian tradition.

Hume believed that man is better defined as a creature of passions, needs, and interests than as a rational being—important as the limited scope of reason is. Having denied that reason is anything but "the slave of the passions," Hume still must account for human action and motivation. Most central to his theory of society and one of the most important aspects of all human operations is sympathy, which according to him involves pleasure and pain with respect to the experiences of other persons [7] and to which a number of functions are ascribed. Sympathy makes men susceptible to the feelings of others and accounts for the relative uniformity of taste and values in any group that gives it the cohesion of a community. Thus, the individual is not in isolation, and furthermore, he inevitably develops the sentiment of sympathy more fully by his association with others.

Moral action and judgment also have their roots in sympathy. Things or human qualities are not good or bad in themselves, nor

[7] Sympathy is produced through the "association of ideas," a doctrine of Hume's psychology, with special reference to pleasure and pain.

could reason, in Hume's view, determine their goodness. Instead, the moral character of acts depends on how men feel about them and the rules that govern them. Moral qualities fall into two groups which Hume called "natural" and "artificial" virtues. Natural virtues are those directly connected with sympathy and appear in personal conduct; artificial virtues rest on the different, though related, motive of enlightened self-love [8] and concern the social sphere, particularly in economic and state matters.

The conventions of morality (a term Hume used that suggests the unprovable status of moral law) are developed with reference to men's permanent interest, and thus they arise out of men's needs. In like manner, society has its basis in the *advantage* of peace and order to mankind. Hume considered the social contract theory false both historically and logically [9] and maintained that it does not account for the origin of society. "Common interest and utility beget infallibly a standard of right and wrong," and no sanction of society and government beyond men's interests is demanded. Hume also denied that society and government, or the principles controlling them, should be called immutable and eternal for they are the result of human nature and its needs.

As the result of men's interests, society and the social virtues like justice that are founded on the grounds of association do not depend, as they do for Hobbes, on the power of government. In a sense, justice and other social virtues are prior to government, not consequent upon it. Men associate naturally and form governments out of their permanent interests, not because of fear and egoistic drives. Hume allowed that if the circumstances are right, men will act virtuously even in the absence of government. This implies finally, also against Hobbes, that the power of government depends on men's assent and obedience, rather than obedience depending on the power of government.

In summary, Hume taught that association is natural to men, that the basis of moral distinctions is men's feelings, that men

[8] This is not Hobbes' universal selfishness, but it is men's permanent interest in government for their own virtue.

[9] Hume thought it probable that government first arose out of quarrels. Utilitarian views on the social contract are discussed more fully in the sections on "State, Power, and Authority" and "The Ideal of Justice."

form governments to secure their long-range interests, that the advantage and utility of civilized society to individuals is the standard for judging particular social actions, and that certain social conventions, like justice, arise to serve and to increase the advantage of society to men.

Problem II: Social and Political Values

The commonly used phrase, "the greatest happiness of the greatest number," interpreted in hedonistic terms, provides a succinct statement of the values to which society and government are to be dedicated for the utilitarian. It calls attention to the maximization of pleasure as a social goal, and it suggests the utilitarian's belief that the only proper meaning of the common good is found in the sum total of individual goods. Yet the phrase also contains some uncertainties, especially when related to the historically developing utilitarian ethical theory.

Two such ambiguities demand special attention. The first is, how to understand "the greatest happiness of the greatest number"? Is the reference of this expression purely quantitative or can pleasures differ in quality as well? While some of the first hedonists were unclear about this question, Bentham was not.[10] He believed that pleasures differed only in quantitative ways such as their duration and extent, and that therefore "the greatest happiness" is a quantitative expression. Since pleasures vary only in this way, Bentham also suggested that they could be predicted and controlled by a quasi-mathematical technique he called the calculus of pleasures. (Prior to Bentham, utilitarianism had not been a "calculating" ethics.) Quantitative determinations of the pleasure or pain consequent upon choices or social policies can be made, and the right choice thereby will be determined for the individual or the legislator.

[10] See Bentham's *Introduction to the Principles of Morals and Legislation.*

It is at this point that John Stuart Mill (1806–1873) made one of his chief modifications of utilitarianism,[11] for Mill found it necessary to assert that pleasures differ in quality as well as in quantity. The pleasures of the mind are distinct in kind from those of the body: "it is better to be a human being dissatisfied than a pig satisfied: better to be Socrates dissatisfied than a fool satisfied." Competent judges, or those who have had education and experience, declare that some pleasures are qualitatively preferable to others, and Mill concluded that their testimony is true.

A second ambiguity in "the greatest happiness of the greatest number" is whether the happiness of the formula is that of individuals who follow only egoistic interests, or whether utilitarianism admits altruistic motives as well. Most utilitarians held a doctrine of psychological as well as ethical hedonism. In addition to defining the good in terms of pleasure, they believed men are *motivated* to seek pleasure and avoid pain. Psychological hedonism seems to imply—though in fact it does not necessitate—an ethical egoism, and many of the early hedonists did hold a theory of egoism. Hume, with his basic notion of sympathy, did not; Bentham was somewhat ambiguous on this point; but John Stuart Mill clearly rejected egoism for an altruistic hedonism. The utilitarian standard, he argued, "is not the agent's own happiness, but the greatest amount of happiness altogether." The standard requires, in fact, strict impartiality between one's own happiness and that of others, and the golden rule contains the complete spirit of the ethics of utility: "to do as you would be done by, and to love your neighbor as yourself, constitute the ideal perfection of utilitarian morality." [12]

Thus while Mill accepted the greatest happiness formula with other utilitarians, his ethical doctrines of altruism and qualitatively distinct pleasures led him to the recognition that certain things— chiefly, freedom and the cultivation of individuality—must be accepted as good in their own right. Mill therefore argued for the freedom of men to form and to express opinions, for freedom of

---

[11] In his widely read *Utilitarianism*.

[12] The question of altruism continues to be an important one in contemporary thought. A valuable recent discussion is found in Thomas Nagel, *The Possibility of Altruism*, Oxford, 1970.

thought, of private judgment, and of discussion. His argument takes two forms, one utilitarian and one that may be called "moral." Observing that mankind is not infallible and has not gained all possible knowledge, and that freedom of thought is a necessary condition for inquiry, Mill argued first that society must grant maximum freedom to individuals in order to further and to protect the pursuit of knowledge. His second argument asserts that the ideal of moral maturity implies that an individual order and judge his life in the light of his own ideas and experiences. Hence, if moral maturity is to be achieved by the members of a society, that society must allow men freedom as a condition of maturity and self-development.

Mill's premises led him to assert further that men must be free not only to form opinions but also to *act* on their own opinions, so long as they do not molest others. The reasons for the two freedoms are the same: men are not infallible and hence unity of opinion is not desirable unless it is the result of full and free comparison of opposite opinions, and diversity is not an evil but a positive good. These reasons led Mill even further, for they imply that in any society there should be both different opinions and different modes of living. It is desirable, then, that individuality and varieties of character should assert themselves when they do not concern others.[13] Human beings are more valuable as their individuality is cultivated, which means that desires and impulses as well as opinions should be one's own. Freedom, self-determination, happiness, individuality: these then are the chief social and political values that Mill developed for the utilitarian tradition.

But, interestingly, the social values Mill supported are not the only ones which can be inferred from utilitarian premises. Writing in the latter half of the nineteenth century, Mill's political judgments were liberal in an individualistic and almost laissez-faire sense. Perhaps paradoxically, what was political liberalism in his

---

[13] Mill attempted to clarify this qualification by a distinction between actions that are private and those that are public. He did not deny that the latter, involving acts that may affect others without their consent, should be regulated by government; he did insist however that government should protect and maintain the autonomy of private acts.

day has become political conservatism in the twentieth century: the two terms have changed places! And with this shift has come a new set of inferences from utilitarianism which suggest that, as happiness is the proper end of life, the power of government should be used in a positive way to fulfill the needs of people and thus support the pursuit of happiness. While Mill would undoubtedly have opposed this position, many contemporary utilitarians have argued for a "welfare state" in which political authority serves human needs and prevents persons from being harmed, sometimes even against their immediate desires.

The philosophic discussion of the welfare state alternative, frequently among utilitarians themselves, is often put in terms of the concept of paternalism.[14] A paternalistic government is one which, in fatherly fashion, supports the happiness of its citizens by preventing harm from befalling them and insuring for them the meeting of their basic needs. A strong paternalism would find value in government policies which do this whether or not citizens agree (the wearing of motorcycle helmets, the required nutrition programs in schools); a weaker paternalism might allow some citizen choice. Needless to say, paternalism itself, as well as its stronger and weaker versions, is a widely debated concept. But it arises as the welfare and happiness of a society, viewed in a utilitarian perspective, are taken as ultimate social values.

Problem III: State, Power, and Authority

Basing their social philosophy on the principle of utility, utilitarians find most of the doctrines of alternative social philosophies to be only "fictions," as Bentham (1748–1832) put it. The social contract, the community, the common good, the separation of powers—these and other notions fall under Bentham's judgment.

---

[14] Some of the best recent work on this issue is found in Joel Feinberg's *Social Philosophy*, Englewood Cliffs, 1973, pp. 45–52.

He tried to describe the nature of political society in terms of interests and habits of obedience, and to understand the "advantage" of society to men in reference to empirical needs and men's desire to obey government.

Utilitarians have generally supported democracy and representative government. Their argument for democracy starts from the greatest happiness principle—it is the right of every man that his happiness shall not count for less than that of anyone else. This implication, together with the assumptions that every man considers his own interests and that he is usually the best judge of them, leads to the principle of the sovereignty of the people. A society of any size, however, could not rule itself in the manner of "pure" democracies, and therefore it is necessary to have a representative scheme where it will be in the people's interest to choose representatives who are anxious to promote all the interests of the people.

Starting as they do from the utilitarian principle rather than natural rights or the common good, these arguments carry further implications about the nature of government. The community is only a "fictitious body" (Bentham), and the interest of the community is but the sum of the interests of those who compose it. Universal suffrage follows from the equal value of every man's happiness, and John Stuart Mill especially worked to achieve this goal as well as the rights of women. The complete sovereignty of the people meant for Bentham that the legislative branch of government should have but one chamber, and that "checks and balances" in government prevent the full working of democracy. His *A Fragment on Government* contains the first effective attack on the doctrine of the separation of powers since it was formulated by Polybius in ancient Greece. Because the satisfaction of human needs is the sole justification of government, Bentham argued that the power of government is effectively to be checked only by the interests of the community.

Writing in opposition to Blackstone,[15] Bentham rejected (as did Hume before him) the fiction of the social contract as the

[15] Sir William Blackstone (1723–1780), perhaps the most famous of English jurists. His *Commentaries* had a great influence in England and America.

basis of government. The doctrine is supposed to provide a basis for just government and for political obligation. In fact, it does neither. If the king be supposed the agent of the people's happiness, how can one determine, asked Bentham, whether he has acted against the people's happiness? There is nothing in the contract to decide this crucial issue. Shall it be decided on the question of whether the king rules according to law?—even though he might make laws against the people's happiness, or he might still rule by law but against happiness. The contract does not fare any better on obligation, for one may question why men ought to keep their promises. An intelligible answer would be that it is to men's advantage to keep them, but then there is no need to speak of obligations following from a contract. Utility alone provides the reason for the existence of authority.

Father of John Stuart Mill and ardent Benthamite, James Mill (1773–1836) also interpreted government as a means to the end of human happiness.[16] The materials needed for happiness are scarce and depend on labor. Therefore, the power of protecting these materials is given to a small group of men, and this is government—a device for protecting men from one another, especially regarding greed for another's property. Government implies power, which is defined by Mill as security in the conformity of the will of one man and the acts of other men. Power, however, is of such a nature that there is no limit to the desire to possess it. The existence of power, therefore, presents a problem that is resolved only by representative government with the right system of checks. And these checks are finally not formal divisions of government, but only the interests of the community itself.

Problem IV: Law and Rights

The chief factors underlying a utilitarian theory of law have now been developed. The critique of ideas and the antimetaphysi-

---

[16] A good source of James Mill's theories is his article on "Government," *Encyclopaedia Britannica*, Supplement to the 5th edition (1815–1818), Vol. 4.

cal temper of utilitarians destroyed the traditional notion that reason reflects a transcendent and eternal Law of Nature. Natural law and right reason are regarded ultimately as subjective fantasies created by the mind itself, with none of the objective validity that had been claimed for them. There being no natural law and right, the utilitarian substitutes human conventions, which, based on the common experience of mankind, are adopted by men because it is in their interest to do so. The variety of human interests and the conflicts that might arise in the search for satisfaction lead men to place themselves under the power of government and to acknowledge it.

A theory of law based upon these factors is developed early in the utilitarian tradition by John Austin (1790–1859).[17] Every positive law, Austin wrote, is set by some sovereign individual or body whose purpose is to confer beneficient rights on individuals in ways conducive to their common happiness. As issued by a sovereign, law takes the form of a command, which is the expression of a desire coupled with the power to inflict pain if the desire is disregarded. The command produces an obligation of obedience because failure to obey may issue in evil (pain). Command and duty are in fact correlative terms, and when coupled with the notion of a sanction, all the elements needed for an understanding of law are present. And insofar as laws are what they ought to be, they are based on utility. Whether they are truly based on utility must be determined, Austin concluded, through observation and induction.[18]

Through these ideas, Austin became the founder of what is usually termed the school of analytic jurisprudence. This school seeks to develop a jurisprudence devoted to the analysis and "censure" (Bentham) of the law in the light of its contribution to the general happiness. The method it follows is generally the construction in clear and logical ways of a system of law based on firm foundations. Austin himself sought to do this in his definition

---

[17] See his *Lectures on Jurisprudence*, ed. Robert Campbell, New York, 1873.
[18] Austin did often write as though the will of God is the ultimate test of laws, while utility is their proximate test. In fact, however, the former has no real juristic significance in Austin's theory, as it did, for example, in medieval theories.

of law as the command of a sovereign. Challenging both natural law theories and metaphysical idealisms, this definition makes sovereignty rather than any ideal of justice the essential element of law. Justice is related externally, not internally, to the definition.[19]

This last observation, together with Austin's emphasis on command and sovereignty, makes it imperative to contrast his views with those of the positivists, particularly in regard to morality and power.[20] Utilitarians differ essentially from Hobbes, for example, in that they distinguish law and morals, and hold that moral rules are not laws. Laws are rules enforced by authority. But is this authority absolute? Utilitarians such as Austin (and Bentham before him) answered that the notion of legal sovereignty does indeed mean a legally unlimited right to make law. Yet complete legal sovereignty does not imply supreme and complete sovereignty, nor does it carry threats to liberty. No direct connection is posited between legal supremacy and obedience; the duties of subject to rulers depend on how they rule. Effective sovereignty, as Hume had already pointed out, rests on a prelegal element, namely the habit of obedience from the bulk of society. Thus, on the one hand, the supreme legislative authority is limited both morally (since the rules of utility never collapse into the definition of law) and in fact (since authority rests on human habits); and on the other hand, in contrast to Montesquieu, the limitation of power by power does not exclude legal supremacy.

---

[19] An external relation is one that makes no difference to, or is not included in, its terms; an internal relation does affect the nature of the terms it relates. Austin suggested that command, duty, and sanction are internally related: each term signifies the same notion, but each denotes a different part of that notion and connotes the rest. Anxious to define law as it is, however, he found it related externally to justice. An unjust law is still a law, though a command without a sanction is not a law.

[20] Yet Austin's work has had tremendous influence on recent positivist schools. In part the reason is that Austin's theory of law is related externally to the principle of utility as to the ideal of justice. The theory can thus be separated from its context and used in the analytic, descriptive ways acceptable to positivists. Further references to this approach are given in Chapter Nine.

PROBLEM V: POLITICAL OBLIGATION

The theory of political obligation that has marked the utilitarian tradition was pretty much laid out by David Hume.[21] "The general obligation, which binds us to government," he wrote, "is the interest and necessities of society; and this obligation is very strong." Thus placing the basis of political obligation in men's general interests for peace and order, Hume spoke of what obliges men to obey government and of what obliges government to serve men by reference to human interests and to the principle of utility that judges them. He distinguished two kinds of duties—natural and artificial. Natural duties such as love and pity, which involve feelings of approval, are based on "natural instinct." The second kind, sometimes called artificial by Hume, are performed from the sense of obligation arising from the necessities of society. So such artificial or social virtues as justice, fidelity, and allegiance become obligatory.

The obligation to society and authority is not a natural instinct, but rather a felt need for social order, and this felt need or interest is sufficient to explain allegiance; no social "fiction" is needed or helpful. The two great theories of authority of his day, hereditary succession and the social contract, were forcefully rejected by Hume. The latter is wanting, Hume found, because the obligation to keep the promises of the contract is no more basic or more easily explained than obedience. They are both on the same level as artificial virtues, and one cannot be used to explain the other. Principles of succession are also wanting as theories of political obligation, since the fact of possessing authority, even for a long time, does not create the obligation to obey. Subjects obey a government, not because of a promise made by their ancestors,

---

[21] See his essays, "Of the Original Contract" and "Of Passive Obedience," in *Essays Moral, Political and Literary*, ed. T. H. Green and T. H. Grose, London, 1875.

nor because a family has possessed the ruling power for generations, but because government is in their interest, and government could not be without obedience. Men approve of what makes for the common interest, they accept the obligations this seems to impose, and thus they make obedience and allegiance virtues.

These virtues are not absolute or unlimited: utilitarians are suspicious of power and absolutisms. Interestingly, while Hume rejected the contract theory, he did not deny the idea of consent. Consent for him is the acquiescence, grounded in knowledge, that government is in the public interest. This means, in effect, that power is the result of obedience, not that obedience is the effect of power, as Hobbes contended. Thus for Hume, consent explains what makes government possible; it is not a principle to explain the grounds of obligation. This is found rather in the interests of society and the principle of utility.

Since the power of government is limited by the motives of obedience that make government possible, it follows that if government is not in men's interest, they cease to obey. In fact, in such circumstances they would have a positive motive for resistance and reform. Resistance being admitted, Hume concluded, the only question can be the degree of necessity that can justify it and "render it lawful or commendable."

PROBLEM VI: THE IDEAL OF JUSTICE

For their existence and comfort men depend on certain products of the earth. These cannot be used in common, however, without certain disputes arising, nor do natural products suffice unless they are improved by human labor. Yet no one works unless he will receive some benefits to himself. Therefore, certain rules arise implying a mutual recognition of rights and the institution of private property. Briefly, such is a general utilitarian account of the origin of the ideal of justice and of its relation to human interests. The notion of an essential Justice discoverable by Reason is abandoned; justice—with allegiance, modesty, and good manners—is treated as an "artificial" virtue in Hume's sense of the term. It is prior to government, it may be appealed to against government, but it is a social rather than an individual virtue because the desire for it arises as men live together. Government is not the maintainer of some eternal, transcendent ideal of justice. It is instead a device that makes it the immediate interest of some persons to serve the general interests of everyone.

Not merely useful, justice for many utilitarians has its character as a virtue determined *wholly* by its usefulness. So understood, justice is the name for certain classes of moral rules concerning the essentials of human well-being, especially as that well-being is specified in human rights and supported by legal sanctions. The rules of justice thus cover such matters as human liberty, equality of rights, desert, impartiality, and they regulate property and rights to property—customary or conventional rights rather than natural ones—in the interest of their stability. (Other conventions have to do with legitimate authority, which rests on rules such as prescription and formal enactment.) Human interests and the utilitarian principle are thus sufficient to account for justice.

Most utilitarian writers have given attention to the concept of justice, and some of the most widely read parts of Hume's and Mill's work have been their chapters on justice. Perhaps the most carefully refined treatment of justice is that by the last great traditional utilitarian, Henry Sidgwick (1838–1900).[22] Sidgwick's contributions to ethical utilitarianism are important and significant, for he sought to show that utilitarianism can admit strictly moral judgments distinct from merely prudential ones. The moral "ought," for Sidgwick, is an irreducible concept.

To develop and maintain this notion, Sidgwick introduced into ethics an intuitive and self-evident element that is cognizable by abstract intuition. He specified this element in terms of three intuitive principles, corresponding to the virtues of prudence, benevolence, and justice. The principle of prudence is that one part of a given conscious experience is not to be regarded, other things being equal, as more important than any other equal part of the same experience. The principle of benevolence considers each

---

[22] See, for example, his *The Methods of Ethics*, 6th edition, London, 1901.

person as morally bound to regard the good of any other person as much as he regards his own. The principle of justice postulates that it cannot be right for A to treat B in a manner in which it would be wrong for B to treat A, merely on the ground that they are two different persons.

The justice of which earlier utilitarians wrote, Sidgwick found, is mainly a theory of order. And the need for order, he admitted, is too obvious to require proof. Sidgwick also agreed that Utility is the principle guiding the meaning of justice. Justice as defined above is a notion more complex than order, and it contains many utilities. Those Sidgwick discussed include impartiality, just claims, normal expectations, and ideal justice, by which he meant the distribution of good and evil according to desert and in relation to happiness. While intuitive principles enter into all his moral and political discussion, Sidgwick nevertheless remained a utilitarian because of his beliefs that pleasure is the only practical test of what is desirable, and that the principle of utility furnishes a common standard for understanding the different components of justice.

While Sidgwick's views are often judged an advance over earlier theories, they have still been unsatisfactory to many recent utilitarians. The basic reason for this is that, for social thought, the concepts of right and justice do not seem firmly grounded. If, for example, the punishment of one innocent person would maximize the happiness of one million others, utilitarianism might be read as suggesting that the punishment is justifiable. But such a consequence, contemporary utilitarians would agree, violates the sense of justice.

To overcome the possibility of paradoxes such as this, a new distinction has been drawn by such thinkers as Richard B. Brandt and David Braybrooke[23] between act utilitarianism and rule utilitarianism. The former, which has been largely the position of traditional utilitarianism, judges human actions as right or wrong as they are conducive to human happiness; but it is just this theory

23 Richard B. Brandt, "Toward a Credible Utilitarianism," in *Morality and the Language of Conduct*, ed. Castaneda and Nakhnikian, Detroit, 1965; and David Braybrooke, *Three Tests For Democracy: Personal Rights, Human Welfare, and Collective Preference*, New York, 1968.

which leads to paradoxes such as that just illustrated above. Any act as means is right if the greater happiness of the greater number results as the end. The introduction of the notion of rules, especially rules of justice and individual rights, however, eliminates such a simplified means-ends schema. Rule utilitarianism rather says, adopt and live under the rule which provides the greatest happiness for the greatest number.[24] Obedience to rules thus determines the rightness of an act like keeping one's promises, while the practice or institution, promise-keeping, is justified on grounds of utility. The so-called paradox of justice is therefore eliminated because the rightness enjoined by the rules cannot be sacrificed to some utilitarian end. Thus the notion of justice, as well as the recognition of human rights, become matters of intrinsic value under rules for an ideal society in which all persons have the best life of which they are capable.[25]

Bibliographical Essay

Most readers will find the primary source materials on utilitarianism easily available and readable, both in respect to its ethical foundations and social philosophy. A number of important descriptive studies are nevertheless available which provide historical perspective and explanation. Standard works include Ernest Albee, *A History of English Utilitarianism*, New York, 1901, reprinted 1962; David Baumgardt, *Bentham and the Ethics of Today*, Princeton, 1952, a valuable book in relating utilitarianism to con-

[24] Brandt's fuller statement is: "An act is right if and only if it conforms with that learnable set of rules the recognition of which as morally binding—roughly at the time of the act—by everyone in the society of the agent except for the retention by individuals of already formed and decided moral convictions, would maximize intrinsic value." This somewhat complicated statement includes the necessary technical refinements of the imperative.

[25] This wording is William K. Frankena's in "Some Beliefs About Justice," in John Bricke, ed., *Freedom and Morality*, Lawrence, Kansas, 1976, p. 69. Frankena does not accept utilitarianism, but his proposal is offered as one acceptable on utilitarian as well as deontological grounds.

temporary thought; William L. Davidson, *Political Thought in England: The Utilitarians from Bentham to J. S. Mill*, London, 1935; Elie Halévy, *The Growth of Philosophical Radicalism*, trans. Mary Morris, London, 1928; G. W. Keeton and G. Schwarzenberger (eds.), *Jeremy Bentham and the Law*, London, 1948; John Plamenatz, *The English Utilitarians*, Oxford, 1949; and Leslie Stephen, *The English Utilitarians*, 3 vols., London, 1900, reprinted 1950. Some anthologies on recent debates concerning utilitarianism have appeared, including that by Smart and Williams, which may also be consulted for further bibliographical material.

Idealism

5

Like many terms used by philosophers, idealism has both a wider and a narrower meaning. Its wider meaning is the one usually used in ordinary speech, and refers to a concern for ideals and sometimes also to a form of commitment to them. If used pejoratively, it may carry the implication that the "idealist" is so involved with his ideals that he overlooks "real" facts in human experience. In the narrower sense, however, idealism denotes a school of philosophy with a technically developed position within which the main arguments deal with ideas rather than ideals. It must be added immediately, however, that this does not mean that idealists have no interest in ideals: they do indeed, often in ways not shared by other philosophers. However, this is their interest as philosophers, not as "common sense" idealists.

With idealism, our study returns to a position within which the metaphysical impulse is strong. Idealism is in fact primarily a metaphysical vision which seeks—like all such visions—to present a coherent, inclusive view of the universe and of man's place within it. Unfortunately, however, it is difficult to provide an accurate and helpful introductory definition of idealism. The word itself is derived from the Greek *idein*, which means to see and also to know. The word goes back further to the Sanskrit root *vid*, to know or to learn. Such an etymology is filled with meanings that center on mind, for only minds or conscious persons can see, know, and learn. This suggests a definition of idealism as the philosophy for which mind, or what is most characteristic of mind, is the fundamental principle of explanation and understanding. As a metaphysics, idealism asserts that the real is mind or the mindlike; as an epistemology, it posits that knowledge is the result of mind's creative activity; and in axiology and related disciplines, it holds the dependency of values on mind. Idealist philosophies thus maintain that the universe, as well as man's experience of it is, in all three respects, the work or embodiment of mind.

While idealists generally accept this description of their position, they do differ in their respective emphases. These differences provide a convenient basis for distinguishing four major varieties of idealism.

First are the mentalists or subjective idealists who, following Bishop George Berkeley (1685–1753), deny the reality of matter and material substances, asserting that physical objects—"all the choir of heaven and furniture of the earth"—are of the same kind of being as is mind itself. A second group of idealists are the absolutists, who urge that certain logical concepts like system or universal best define reality, and that reality so characterized is one inclusive mindlike structure. In other words, knowledge, value, and the universe are most adequately understood when viewed in terms of such notions as systematic interrelation or the manifestation of universals. A third school of idealists seeks to discover the presuppositions or "transcendental conditions" (Kant) of experience, which they profess to find in mind and its activities. To know some particular fact, for example, is to know it as a kind of fact with relations to other facts, which presupposes the mental activities of classification and systematization. Among the presuppositions of factual knowledge, therefore, are these acts of mind. Finally, there are idealist philosophers who argue that values are in some sense objective and part of the nature of reality. Yet, because value implies mind—apart from mind there is no experience of, nor meaning to, value—they draw the idealist conclusion that reality is in its essence spiritual.

At the risk of some repetition, it may be helpful for understanding these idealistic assertions to survey briefly some of the major arguments for them. One such argument—in fact, group of arguments—attempts to show that knowledge of anything implies that it is relative to mind. Consider what is meant by a fact of experience, either taken simply or as part of the systems of science, art, or morality. Facts are always found within a set of relationships held together by consciousness. Thus, relationship presupposes a self-distinguishing consciousness—a consciousness of system or relation—that functions as a principle of synthesis uniting phenomena in a single, inclusive universe. Knowledge is a function of the human mind, to be sure; but the knowability of the universe—even of any single fact—implies that an objective spiritual principle, a Cosmic or Absolute Mind, is fundamental to and constitutes the reality of the universe.

Closely related to this epistemological argument is one based on value experience. For some idealists, in fact, the preceding argument is only a part of the larger problem of values. They urge that reason, if abstracted from ideals and values like system, coherence, truth, and intelligibility, is incapable of discharging its function of grasping reality. Only an ideal world, a world that embodies and fulfills man's ideals, is knowable and intelligible. This means that ideals are objective, for they form the structure (or part of the structure) of reality itself. In support of this conclusion, idealists assert that while the experience of value is "subjective" because it is always an experience of persons, there is also in that experience an "objective reference" to the claim that values *ought* to be appreciated whether or not one actually does appreciate them. The ground for holding the objectivity of value on the basis of this reference is that men's value judgments can be organized into an intelligible system when such judgments are interpreted as claims that reality makes upon men. However, a reality laying claims on men must itself be ideal, a spiritual principle that is both ultimate reality and the locus of ideals.

Through arguments of these kinds, idealists are led to posit an eternal consciousness or spiritual being as the ultimate reality.[1]

---

[1] There are two refinements here that students of the metaphysics of idealism may wish to pursue. One is the distinction between monism or absolutism, which views the universe ultimately as one mind, and pluralisms, which hold that the real consists of many minds. The other refinement concerns personal and impersonal idealism, which reflects the differing emphases of idealists on the mental or conscious nature of the Absolute.

This conclusion, however, is also built on the negative argument that any belief in matter or material substance existing independent of mind is unjustified. Thinking, willing, knowing: activities such as these make up human experience, and what we experience is always something within the framework of experience. No reality, idealists argue, can be admitted that does not fall within this framework. To be realities, things must be constituted within the system of relationships that, as was seen above, is supported by a spiritual principle. A completely independent reality, a reality totally unrelated to mind, is not only unknowable, but indeed unthinkable. Of course, the idealist does not argue that reality is limited to *human* experience: he is saying that to be real is to be an element in experience as such, the experience of the Absolute.

Idealist arguments are frequently difficult to follow at a first reading. They often appear to contradict what seems to be common sense in addition to being abstract and technical. Perhaps it will be helpful to say in summary that idealist arguments lead to the following basic assertions: the world of ordinary perceptual experience is not the real world—reality is a *spiritual* principle beyond everyday experience; ideals are objective and part of the real itself; and reality, since it embodies ideals, is knowable and intelligible.[2]

The social philosophy of the great idealists is developed within this guiding metaphysical position. The task of philosophy, they argue, is to seek to know the various standards and values, ends and purposes, of human life; and this same task confronts the philosopher as he examines society. Working with their conceptions of reason, personality, and ideals, idealists find in man a fundamental social impulse that is also a moral impulse to achieve the ideal. When rightly organized, society tries to give this impulse realization in a form adequate to the full and ideal meaning of morality. And when rightly understood, idealistic theories of rationality, of ethics, and of society are interrelated if not identical.

[2] See W. M. Urban's summary in *Beyond Realism and Idealism*, London, 1949, which is valuable for its discussion of these points.

The discussions which follow develop the idealistic perspective in terms of its distinctive emphasis in social philosophy.

Problem I: Man and Society

For idealists, the heading "man and society" raises questions about the nature of human personality, the meaning of community, and the relationship between the two—matters to be examined within the framework of idealistic metaphysical assumptions. From that metaphysics come such ideas as purpose, ideal selfhood, self-realization, reason, and consciousness, all of which are peculiarly relevant to the idealist's understanding of the human condition. Their meaning for a theory of man will be explained first.

As was seen in the introduction above, knowledge is explained in idealistic theory on the supposition that facts are related in a system held together by consciousness; man is capable of knowledge because he is a being conscious of facts. In a similar way, man is viewed as capable of conduct or morality because he is conscious of objects and deeds. For something to be an object means that it is related to some desire. Moral action [3] occurs when a person identifies himself with an object of desire, thus seeking to fulfill a purpose, to make real the idea of some better state of being, and to satisfy himself.

In this explanation of human action, consciousness is the critical point. Even the most objectless human life, idealists insist, forms a system in which particular desires meet and are qualified by the conception of something desirable on the whole. In so forming even an elementary system, desires are also permeated by reason. And, since objects and desires are related to consciousness and reason, the system they constitute points toward completion

---

[3] This expression as used here is largely descriptive. It means action capable of being judged in reference to some moral criterion. The idealist's criterion for normative judgment is given in the following paragraphs.

in an "ideal self" that serves as both goal and judge of individual conduct. The ethical task for each person is to realize the ideal self in his own life, thus to achieve full "self-realization," as the theory is commonly named.[4]

Idealists find that society also is best represented as a system that depends on the recognition of something desirable on the whole, of the "common good," that involves other persons and is at the same time one of the sources of true self-satisfaction for the individual. The moral impulse is a social impulse: man is conscious of himself as an end to himself, yet because he is so aware of himself, he also has consciousness of others similarly conceived. The social impulse is also moral, for society tries to support this impulse in a form adequate to the full meaning of self-realization. Thus, to paraphrase the English idealist, T. H. Green: social life is to human personality what language is to thought; for language presupposes thought as a capacity, but this capacity is actualized only in language. Similarly, society presupposes persons in capacity or potency, but it is only in the intercourse of men, when they recognize each other as ends, not merely as means, and thus have reciprocal claims, that the capacity is actualized and men truly live as persons. To function in support of self-realization, every society rests on the reality of some shared and acknowledged conception of a good common to all its members. The spiritual principle of consciousness is the source of this common good, and human society is ultimately an achievement of rationality.

The conditions of community, as idealists develop them, reflect these idealistic teachings.[5] A community is neither a mere collection of individuals nor simply cooperative activities. Persons constitute a community by reference to an ideal past and future that makes them members of a "spiritual body" whose activities are "the life of my own self writ large." The existence of com-

---

[4] Self-realization is also the name frequently associated with Aristotle's ethics, to which many idealists are heavily indebted. The latter, however, lay greater stress than Aristotle did on the relation of the ideal to consciousness and—as will be seen more fully in the discussion of law and rights—on mutual recognition for the analysis of rights.

[5] A clear and important source of these conditions is Josiah Royce (1855–1916), *The Problem of Christianity*, 2 vols., New York, 1913.

munities depends on the power of the self to extend its life to past and future through deeds done and ends sought, on social communication, and on the identity of some events experienced by all members of the community. While thus rooted in human nature and needs, society is also one of the conditions of that realization of selfhood that is the moral ideal.

PROBLEM II: SOCIAL AND POLITICAL VALUES

The idealist's teleological view of man and society reflects a set of values involved in the ideal of self-realization. This ideal is one of personal worth: "all other values are relative to value for, of, or in a person" (T. H. Green). So act, Immanuel Kant (1724–1804) said, that you treat humanity, whether in your own person or in that of another, always as an end in itself, never merely as a means. This is a dictate of reason, which serves as the basis of a theory of society because it is the source of practical rules serving the common interest and of self-imposed subjection to these rules. Human communities are thus founded on the unity of consciousness with its capacity to grasp the idea of a common, permanent good and the duties it implies.

Immanuel Kant's writings provide a guide for following the idealistic theory of social values.[6] Unlike most subsequent idealists, Kant accepted a version of the social compact theory to account for the nature of society, though he qualified the theory to such an extent that it is hardly recognizable. In no way does the compact refer to historic fact: it is an "idea of reason" signifying the union of wills that is the original condition for the existence of any society. This union of men must be viewed as an end in itself so that every person ought to carry it out as a primary and unconditional duty. This primary and unconditional duty is the realization of the capacities and rights of men under compulsory laws.

[6] Important essays are conveniently collected in *Kant's Principles of Politics*, tr. W. Hastie, Edinburgh, 1891.

According to Kant, reason wills that a commonwealth be a relation of free men who live under law, a relation that is based on three rational principles of value that serve as the presuppositions making the commonwealth possible. The first principle is the *liberty* of every member of society as a man—a principle first in importance as well as in order. Idealists generally take freedom to be a "positive" conception. It is not just freedom from the interference of others, but a positive power of doing or enjoying something worth doing or enjoying. To do things worth doing means to act as one ought, to act rationally, and to be disciplined in discharging moral obligations. The "external right" of liberty arises out of this notion of human freedom, for "right" involves the limitation of the action of an individual to agree with the freedom of others.

The second principle is the *equality* of every member of society as a subject. Kant wrote of legal and civil equality, not of social equality. In fact, he believed that legal equality is compatible with inequality of talents and possessions. As subjects, all persons must be compelled or coerced only by public law, and they may resist unlawful coercion by the same means.

The third rational principle of society is the *self-dependency* of every member as a citizen. Here Kant meant that every qualified person must be considered equal in giving or enacting laws. A public law, he argued, is an act of a public will, and hence only the will of a whole people is competent to legislate for the whole. No particular will can be legislative rightfully for a commonwealth; liberty, equality, and the public will all require the independent (or self-dependent) participation of citizens in the formulation of rules for the public domain.

It is not a great oversimplification to view the idealistic theory of social values as a set of implications from the ethical theory of self-realization. No other person, no law, no society can be the agent of one's own conduct: moral action is always self-originating and a product of one's own will. But there are certain external conditions that must be fulfilled in order that individual self-realization may occur. These conditions—which may be called moral because they are necessary to self-realization—are the values defining the *telos* or purpose of society as well as, *mutatis mutandis*, of individual life.

PROBLEM III: STATE, POWER, AND AUTHORITY

Idealists argue that human beings achieve maturity and self-realization only in communal life. Man is indeed a social animal. In communities, however, there is a special institution called the state that has a distinctive role to fill in relation to self-realization. One of the most widely studied, as well as debated even among idealists, accounts of the state is that of G. W. F. Hegel (1770–1831).

To understand Hegel's theory, it is necessary to introduce one of his most central conceptions, namely the dialectic. This term refers to his understanding of change and development, which he analyzed in a threefold series of stages called thesis, antithesis, and synthesis. The thesis in any change is its starting point, or that from which the change ensues. The thesis is "abstract" in Hegel's view, for it is undifferentiated and separated from its relations. The antithesis is "other" than the thesis, related to the thesis and yet different from it. The third stage of change is the synthesis, which develops out of the difference and tension between thesis and antithesis. The synthesis cancels out both thesis and antithesis, yet it also preserves them in a higher unity. A synthesis is also more "concrete" because it is differentiated and includes more relations. Hegel taught that all reality is dialectical in this sense: dialectic is the law both of thought and of being.

The dialectic is illustrated in Hegel's *Philosophy of Right*, his basic writing in social philosophy. In this book Hegel attempted to show that society advances by continually making adjustments to the tensions created by internal factors. An overall triad is developed, consisting of abstract right, morality, and ethical life. The thesis, abstract right, is the level of life on which sheer individualism—individual wills—is asserted. The mere conflict of individuals tends to be destructive, so there is movement to the antithesis, morality, in which men are viewed as the bearers of rights and obligations. Even this level, however, is abstract and partial, for it omits all reference to society and men's dependence on it. Hence arises the synthesis, communal life, in which individual and society are interrelated and mutually dependent.

Within communal life a second triad—family, civil society, and the state—is developed by Hegel. Men find themselves socially organized first in family units. These break down, however, because of their inadequacy to the whole range of human interests—they are "abstract." An antithesis therefore develops, namely civil society, which is the realm of "blind inclination" and motivation by interests. But civil society is also inadequate for it depends on some higher institution to give it supervision and moral significance. This institution is the state, which is the synthesis of the triad. "Higher" than civil society, the state thus comes into being with genuine public authority. It seeks to establish an ethical order by action in obedience to conscious ends.

Hegel made a number of different assertions about the state. It is the actuality of the ethical idea, meaning that the state maintains the conditions for the realization of the communal ethical life. Among the highest human needs is the need to participate in causes and purposes larger than private wants and satisfactions; only life in the state can provide such a social cause.[7] Perhaps Hegel's meaning can be made clearer by contrasting his view with philosophical liberalism. As Hegel understood it, liberalism fails to recognize that the citizen's personality is a social nature that must participate in the life of civil society and in the state as a condition of its moral significance. In this failure, liberalism falsifies the notion of social institutions; it regards them as accidental to the moral and spiritual development of personality. In the same vein, Hegel spoke of the state as objective mind. Conceptions of the state for other thinkers—Bentham or Hume, for example—would be inadequate for Hegel because they recognize only the

---

[7] Hegel did not make social life the highest value: art, religion, and philosophy are yet more fulfilling activities.

pursuit of private ends, or argue that all ends are private. But Hegel taught that private ends, which belong to the sphere of civil society, ultimately have no meaning apart from a social context of public ends needed for their realization. The state must coordinate private and public, particular and universal (substantial) interests, a coordination that led Hegel to see the state as rational.

Finally, Hegel spoke of the state as the actuality of concrete freedom. Freedom for Hegel and many idealists is the ability to do what one deliberately chooses to do, and this positive ability is conceivable only for creatures who live in a moral order. Here again we met the idealist insistence on the connection between individual realization and the external conditions that support it. Only after a man is a moral being, after he has acquired some values, can he rationally prefer some of his impulses to others. Otherwise he is but a slave to his impulses, unable to control or select from among them. Freedom is the supreme value for spirit, and the state, Hegel concluded, is the highest type of community in which spirit is made actual.

A frequently repeated charge against Hegel as well as some other idealists which deserves special mention is that his theory leads to political absolutism. One answer to this charge has been provided by the English idealist, Bernard Bosanquet (1848–1923).[8] Hegel, to whom Bosanquet frequently referred, did find the unity of the state to be expressed ultimately in its sovereignty, and also occasionally used the term absolute, though he never meant by it "arbitrary." Writing without the apparatus of the dialectic, Bosanquet attempted to clarify the idealistic doctrine of the state by describing it as the "guardian of the whole moral world": it seeks to maintain the external conditions of the good life for all its citizens; and behind any use of force lies the general (rational) will. If absolutism is taken to mean a theory of an all-powerful state which acts in arbitrary ways against its citizens, then the term in no way applies to idealistic social philosophies, including Hegel's. But, in fact, neither more nor less government is the basic issue, Bosanquet concluded; the basic issue is to have the best government.

[8] See his *Social and International Ideals*, London, 1917.

PROBLEM IV: LAW AND RIGHTS

Idealists attempt to present their philosophy of law through a series of inferences from the self-consciousness of a reasonable being. Self-conscious and possessing the capacities of will and reason, man is also a moral being. His moral ideals remain abstract, however, until he lives in a society whose institutions embody the conditions for their realization. It is civil life that "gives reality" to man's personal capacities and makes their concrete exercise possible. Thus, idealists are led to argue that only the teleological view of man and society can provide an adequate theory of law and rights.

While law has its ground in man's moral capacities, ethics and law must be sharply distinguished. Legality relates to external human acts that can conform to some standard set by law; ethics concerns internal acts of will and motives. In fact, not even all external acts are within the province of legal obligations, but only those that must be regulated in order that the moral end of self-realization may be made possible to citizens. Thus, law is the rules issued and sanctioned by civil authority to order those actions of men related to the maintenance of the possibility of moral development.

As has been seen, however, idealists argue that the true political community does not consist in power alone: it is an organization in which men are clothed with rights and duties and come to be conscious of their obligations. Once again, it is consciousness that makes possible the recognition of rights, which are of the same metal as law—in fact, the other side of the same coin. A right, as T. H. Green (1836–1882) developed his idealistic theory,[9] has two elements: a claim to freedom of action in order to realize one's inner powers and capacities; and the general social

---

[9] *Lectures on the Principles of Political Obligation*, in *Works of Thomas Hill Green*, 3 vols., New York, 1886.

recognition that the claim is warranted, that the individual's freedom contributes to the general good. Thus idealists argue that there must be rights because moral personality ought to be developed, and the possession of rights, ascribed and guaranteed to individuals by law and the state, is the condition of that development. The second element in Green's view means that one has rights only in a society where some common good is recognized by the members of society as their own ideal good.[10] To summarize, then: the existence of rights ascribed to members of a community depends on moral personality, on the recognition by each of the moral personality of others, and on the consciousness by all of common interests and objects.

Such a view of rights involves a rejection of traditional theories of natural rights. As Green put it, a law is good because it contributes to the realization of certain ends, not because it conforms to antecedent natural rights. Not natural law, but the "naturalness of law" is Green's view: if rights are still termed natural, it is "not in the sense that they actually exist when a man is born and that they have existed as long as the human race, but that they arise out of, and are necessary for the fulfillment of, a moral capacity without which a man would not be a man." The so-called law of nature, understood as an ethical law, must be based on consciousness. Only when men are conscious of it are they bound by it. But then, Green argued, it ceases to be a law of nature. In a similar way, Green rejected the notion of consent developed by liberals: the moral end, not consent, is the ground of law, rights, and the state itself.

PROBLEM V: POLITICAL OBLIGATION

According to some authorities, for example Professor A. P. D'Entrèves, the idealist T. H. Green was the first philosopher to

---

[10] Strictly speaking, this interdependence of claim and recognition is an ethical rather than a juristic or legal conception.

use the phrase "political obligation." While this does not at all mean that the problem of political obligation was absent from previous theories, it does suggest that idealists have isolated this problem and given it special attention. Green's own theory of obligation—followed by many idealists—always referred to man's purpose or goal present in his consciousness as the form of his ideal self. Man's capacity to grasp a common idea of a permanent good, a common or rational good, is presupposed in all groupings of men; it is in relation to this good that the source of political obligation is to be found.

Briefly put, the idealist theory is this: men have a common moral end that is the object of their permanent interest and rational will. The state is a device to help men realize this object; its authority—and men's obligation to it—therefore rests on the state's being necessary to that end. What this means is that men's rights, which have been seen to be the conditions of self-realization guaranteed by the state, do not depend on conventions or contracts, nor simply on a sovereign power, nor again on men's individual interests or immediate desires; they derive from that good which is common to all men and which defines their fulfillment and realization. As the instrument and protector of the common good, the state has rights against or over its citizens: it can compel them in their external actions to maintain the order dictated by the common good. Yet citizens are obliged to obey the state because it is the agent of their rational will or common good. Four propositions support and amplify this obligation: [11] (1) there is a distinction between the immediately experienced and the rational will, (2) the rational will is the same for all men, (3) men's common end is the basis of their rights, and (4) the justification of the state lies in furthering this end.

But does the state have obligations to its citizens? Or, what amounts to the same thing, can a citizen ever disobey his government? In general, idealists answer these questions affirmatively. Insofar as a state fulfills the idea of a state, there is no right to disobey it. But the state is an instrument, a means; it is obliged to

[11] For a statement of an idealistic theory of obligation and of these propositions, see Brand Blanshard (1892–   ), *Reason and Goodness*, London, 1961.

maintain the common good. Should a state become so corrupt that it cuts men off from their proper ends, it not only may, sometimes it must be disobeyed. And yet the idealist would point out that the appeal to disobedience involves the same end as obedience, namely the common good. The general principle that one should always act as a citizen does not mean that one must always conform to the laws of his state. It does mean, however, that all assertions against the state must be founded on an acknowledged common and social good.

Problem VI: The Ideal of Justice

The various positions taken by idealists on the fundamental questions of social philosophy reflect concerns for personality, conscience and morality, and the "ideal" element in man's experience. All of these come together in the discussion of justice, the consummate political value and goal. One important presentation of this view which can serve as a guide for presenting an idealistic theory of justice is found in the writings of Sir Ernest Barker (1874–1960).[12] Influenced especially by T. H. Green, Barker was a distinguished English historian and analyst of political ideas. Though he was not an idealistic metaphysician, his own constructive efforts in social philosophy give expression to the idealist perspective.

Justice, Barker wrote, is "the reconciler and the synthesis of political values: it is their union in an adjusted whole." Justice is thus a term of synthesis, allotting to persons their rights. It seeks to balance and to reconcile the conflicting claims of persons and principles, and thus to produce that right order of right relations that guarantees to all persons the external conditions of their development.

But what is the source of this ideal term of synthesis? Some philosophers, including realists, have suggested that nature or es-

[12] See his *Principles of Social and Political Theory*, Oxford, 1951.

sence is such a source. Nature will not do, however, for idealists insist that the ground of obligations and ideals must be, not something which is, but something which is itself ideal. Nor can that source be economics, as Marxists will insist in the next chapter: economic analysis may uncover descriptive laws of economic behavior but cannot uncover the meaning of the total and controlling ideal that justice is. Again, justice (and law) cannot be viewed as a "minimum morality" of a people, for justice aims not at some minimum but at the highest and best, namely a human and social space in which moral energies and development may freely occur.

The last observation, however, gives a clue to the source of justice for idealism. It is an ethical source, typically stated in Kantian terms as the intrinsic worth of persons. Respect for personality is the basis and origin of social thought just as, and just because, it is the basis of ethical thought. The end of society, idealists have argued, is thus to foster the highest possible development of all the capacities of all its members, and the ideal of justice is therefore an ideal of the "right ordering" of social relations among persons to achieve that end.

Statements such as these, and perhaps many others throughout this section on idealism, may raise further questions about the relationship of ethics and law, a relationship whose clarification may aid the understanding of the conception of justice. The source of the principle of justice, idealists assert, is ethics in the sense that justice is a kind of moral standard of the community, reinforced by the general moral conscience. Law, which is the impersonal expression of justice, has validity through declaration, recognition, and enforcement; it has value through its expression of the demands of moral conscience in the form of a rule of right for human relations. Given that ethics is thus the source of justice, in what sense is the state a moral agent? Fundamentally, it must be recognized that law *is not* ethics: ethics deals with inner motives; law can deal only with external acts, or acts that external sanctions can secure. This distinction means that it is impossible that the state be the actual agent of its citizens' morality.

Justice, with the state, rather supports the development of persons through "partnership" with them. And this it does because, as Green put it, all good is for, of, and in persons; and because the intrinsic value of personality is the basis of all political thought. So based, justice is the "joining" of persons and principles as the expression of the final and ultimate social value. And as an ideal it is not simply given in human society but is rather a goal to be sought and won in the concrete, reflective strivings of human society.

Bibliographical Essay

For purposes of introduction to basic idealistic arguments, two surveys of idealism by Josiah Royce are important, *Lectures on Modern Idealism*, New Haven, 1919, reprinted 1964 and, in the relevant chapters, *The Spirit of Modern Philosophy*, New York, 1892. An anthology edited by A. C. Ewing, *The Idealistic Tradition*, Glencoe, Ill., 1957, presents an interesting collection of papers and includes a bibliography that readers may consult for intensive study in idealism. An introductory text covering idealism is E. S. Brightman and Robert N. Beck, *An Introduction to Philosophy*, 3d ed., New York, 1963. Somewhat more advanced are discussions of idealism in such books as Clifford Barrett (ed.), *Contemporary Idealism in America*, New York, 1932; G. W. Cunningham, *The Idealistic Argument in Recent British and American Philosophy*, New York, 1933; A. C. Ewing, *Idealism: A Critical Survey*, London, 1934; and John Howie and Thomas O. Buford (eds.), *Contemporary Studies in Philosophical Idealism*, Cape Cod, 1975.

The social philosophy of idealism and major idealists is treated in such works as: M. B. Foster, *The Political Philosophy of Plato and Hegel*, Oxford, 1935; Norman Wilde, *The Ethical Basis of the State*, Princeton, 1924; Francis B. Harman, *The Social Philosophy of the St. Louis Hegelians*, New York, 1943; John E. Smith, *Royce's Social Infinite*, New York, 1950; A.J.M. Milne, *The Social Philosophy of English Idealism*, London, 1962; T. M. Knox, trans., *Hegel's Political Writings*, Oxford, 1964; Melvin Richter, *The Politics of Conscience: T. H. Green and His Age*, Cambridge, Mass., 1964; Peter Fuss, *The Moral Philosophy of Josiah Royce*, Cambridge, Mass., 1965; and G. A. Kelley, *Idealism, Politics and*

History: Sources of Hegelian Thought, Cambridge, 1969. Special studies of Hegel, including his social theories, have recently been appearing with great frequency; among them are: Z. A. Pelczynski (ed.), *Hegel's Political Philosophy: Problems and Perspectives*, Cambridge, 1971; Shlomo Avineri, *Hegel's Theory of the Modern State*, Cambridge, 1972; Charles Taylor, *Hegel*, Cambridge, 1975; and Judith N. Shklar, *Freedom and Independence*, Cambridge, 1976. A somewhat neglected but still important idealist social philosophy was developed by R. G. Collingwood in *The New Leviathan*, Oxford, 1942.

Current work on all aspects of idealism can be followed in the journal *Idealistic Studies*.

CHAPTER 6

Communism

Together with his collaborator, Friedrich Engels (1820–1895), and his successor, V. I. Lenin (1870–1924), Karl Marx (1818–1883) is the founder of one of the most influential philosophies in the modern world. Born in Trier in West Germany, he showed a deep interest in culture early in life. His education was at first directed toward a career in law, but by 1839 he wished to become a professor of philosophy. His studies in philosophy included the works of Spinoza, Leibniz, Hume, Kant, Feuerbach, and above all, Hegel. In 1841 at Jena, Marx submitted his dissertation, a study of the differences in the materialism of Democritus and Epicurus. Almost immediately, however, he developed deep and abiding interests in social problems. In 1842 he met Engels, a man whose mind was the same as his (Marx and Engels never differed on theoretical matters), and from then until his death in 1883, he worked as a writer and organizer for the communist movement.

The social interests Marx developed were rooted in his sympathy for the proletarian (workers') revolution of his century. One of the keenest social observers, Marx saw that capitalism as an economic institution was producing a class of men who live solely from their wages. That is, workers were becoming little more than commodities, selling themselves on the labor market and relating themselves to society merely through a "cash nexus." Political relations such as power and law that control the social life of the proletariat are but reflections of the capitalist economic structure, and they served to maintain the servile and inhuman condition of the working class. Yet, Marx insisted, capitalism need not be ac-

cepted as the necessary economic system for Europe: it is not the
result of timeless economic laws, as some of its theorists insisted.
Marx saw capitalism as a phase in historical evolution that can be
surpassed if conditions are right. Such an insight, Marx himself
realized, contains the seeds of a revolutionary movement, and he
set about to create a social philosophy for the rising proletariat and
for the revolutionary role that he believed the proletariat would
take.

That philosophy is historical or dialectical materialism. The
term dialectical reminds one of Hegel, and communism is indeed
unthinkable apart from Hegel. That history is a process, that historical process is patterned in terms of thesis-antithesis-synthesis,
that the driving force of the dialectical process is tension and
opposition, and that the dialectic moves toward an "end" that
reconciles the conflicts of preceding stages: these notions were all
accepted by Marx. Yet Marx was at the same time critical of Hegel,
for the dialectic must move in the realm of real forces, not logical
abstractions. It is necessary, he said, to turn Hegel "right way up,"
and this he did in terms of his materialism. By materialism Marx
meant economic determinism, which is the view that the process
of economic production is the basic force in history and society.
The character of production determines the character of social life
because it makes social life possible and creates the need for social
institutions.

This union of dialectic with materialism transformed Hegel-
ianism into a revolutionary radicalism. Marx found what he took
to be a revolutionary element in Hegel himself, particularly in the
latter's dialectical treatment of religion, which implied that the
so-called absolute truths of particular religions are in fact relative
to religious evolution. Generalizing from this application, Marx
made economics a historical science as well, and thus he interpreted
various economies such as feudalism and mercantilism as relative
stages in economic evolution.

As Marx saw it, the history of the modern world can be
understood in terms of a general triad whose thesis is feudalism,
whose antithesis is capitalism, and whose synthesis is—or will be
—communism. Though feudalism did not "depersonalize" labor

as capitalism does, it had to be transcended because of its low productive capacities. Capitalism therefore emerged, and with it came high levels of production. (Marx did not deny the value of economic growth in capitalistic economies.) However, it also brought a number of evils, including the exploitation of man by man and the alienation of man from himself. Therefore, a higher synthesis is needed, which will retain the productivity of capitalism, yet eliminate its disvalues; and this Marx sketched in his ideal of the classless communist society.

The formulation of the theory of historical materialism belongs to the earlier part of Marx's career; his concern with economics—including his detailed critique of capitalism—belongs to the latter part. Neither Marx nor Engels was a systematic philosopher in the sense of an Aristotle or a Hume, that is, in the sense of a systematic critic of the ideas men use to explain their world or their actions. They did not make any significant contributions to basic areas of philosophy such as metaphysics or epistemology, and they insisted that "philosophers have only interpreted the world differently—the main thing is to change it." They did offer, however, a philosophic interpretation of society and of the values and disvalues men may experience in society. The sections below seek to develop the details of that interpretation.

PROBLEM I: MAN AND SOCIETY

The fundamental assertion of dialectical materialism is that the system of production in any society determines the society's structure and the cultural institutions erected on it. Even man's consciousness is so determined. Does it require deep intuition, Marx asked, "to comprehend that man's ideas, views and conceptions, in one word, man's consciousness, changes with every change in the conditions of his material existence, in his social relations, and in his social life?" The question, of course, is only rhetorical, but to understand it fully requires linking this deterministic theory with another Marxist thesis, namely that "the history of all hitherto existing society is the history of class struggles."

The notion of class is a crucial element in Marx's view of man's social condition.[1] "Class" for Marx is a limited and economically determined concept: the class to which a man belongs depends on whether he owns property, and if so, what kind. Under capitalism, for example, the bourgeoisie constitutes one class, namely that which owns the means of production and distribution; and the proletariat is a second, distinct class because it is propertyless. So understood, class is Marx's replacement for Hegel's state as the unit of history, and the dialectic moves through the relations between classes. In turn, Marx made two further assumptions about classes: the relation between them is one of antagonism, and a single class always dominates and is the exploiter of all other classes. Antagonism and domination mark the existence of classes, Marx insisted, because the interests of conflicting classes are irreconcilable. Class interests arise out of, and are relative to, the economic situations of classes, and from these diverse interests come diverse notions of justice, of morality, of religion—in short, of different *ideologies.*

This last conception is one of Marx's most interesting ideas. By an ideology he meant the "superstructure" or system of ideas, especially normative ones, which reflects underlying economic realities and which is developed, not to explain the world (this task belongs to science), but to support class interests and social conditions. Because this is their function, Marx spoke of ideologies as "false consciousness" and as "illusion," though this does not mean that he denied their influence or authority.[2] The opposite is true; established social relations are defended by the economically privileged class whose ideology is reflected in them. But Marx insisted that, for economic determinism,

[1] Many references to Marx can be given for these citations. On "class" see, for example, the *Manifesto of the Communist Party,* and on materialism see the Preface to A *Contribution to the Critique of Political Economy.*

[2] Engels, it may be noted, divided ideology into (1) science and technology and (2) law, morals, art, philosophy, and religion. Only the second is termed by him false consciousness.

> *morality, religion, metaphysics, all the rest of ideology and their corresponding forms of consciousness, thus no longer retain the semblance of independence. They have no history, no development; but men, developing their material production and their material intercourse, alter, along with their real existence, their thinking and products of their thinking. Life is not determined by consciousness but consciousness by life.*

But "life" or economic reality does not always determine consciousness in ways consistent with man's fundamental capacities or, as Marx termed them, his species-being. This is especially true of the present conflict of bourgeoisie and proletariat within capitalism. Neither capitalism nor the ideology of the bourgeoisie is adequate to the meaning of human personality. In fact, man finds himself *alienated* from both self and society, because society sets up standards of behavior through its dominant ideology, yet it at the same time produces motives that move men to reject those standards. Incompatible passions arise that conflict with one another and with the rules and values men are taught to accept. They feel themselves to be rootless and impelled to take courses of action that are unsatisfying. Crime, disobedience, and sometimes destructive violence accompany this alienated condition.

Yet alienation need not be. To be sure, Marx said, great social changes must occur before a society adequate to human nature will emerge. Man is a creature whose view of himself—indeed, his very nature—and of his world is a product of what he does to satisfy his needs. As the only animal who works, man makes himself, so to speak, through his work. He is also a creature who can come to understand himself and his world. Through understanding and by working on his environment, man can be "made whole" again. Alienation will end when man brings his passions into harmony with his values and his ambitions into relation to the means at his disposal.[3]

---

[3] This point is relevant to Marx's treatment of religion. As indicated above, religion is ideology or false consciousness. It functions for alienated man as a comforter or opiate. So interpreted, however, religion will disappear in the ideal society where alienation is overcome.

PROBLEM II: SOCIAL AND
POLITICAL VALUES

The Marxist position on social values contains some ambiguity, if not in its sources in Marx and Engels, at least among some interpreters. Reflecting the scientific, even positivist emphasis in Marx, some Marxists have insisted that the problems in repressive societies are primarily factual ones: exploitation is a fact, alienation is a fact. Eschewing value theory, these communists have argued —perhaps in following Marx's injunction that new theories are not needed for the world, the point is to change it [4]—that an understanding of social facts and the social laws covering them is the essential philosophical activity, and this understanding is one of the instruments of social change. Marx may have given a further basis for this emphasis in his belief that "communism is for us not a *state* which ought to be established, an *ideal* to which reality will have to adjust itself." [5]

Other interpreters, however, find a moral stance in much of communist literature that places it within the moralistic tradition of political philosophy. Both in its critiques and its positive suggestions, this tradition works in relation to moral values and ideals, attempting to judge and to propose for society ways in which to promote those values. To be sure, individual thinkers have their various and differing value systems as has been seen in some of the preceding sections, but Marx agreed with Plato, St. Thomas, Locke, and a host of others that moral criticism of society is an essential part of the philosopher's work.

Whether viewed in a "factual" or "ideal" way, then, this value system may be approached through its analysis of capitalism, and Marx criticized capitalism as much on valuational as on economic

[4] The Eleventh of the *Theses on Feuerbach*.
[5] From *The German Ideology*.

grounds. The key term in this criticism is *exploitation*, which is the appropriation by the bourgeoisie of the surplus value produced by workers.[6] In turn, the notion of surplus value is related to the labor theory of value, which Marx accepted from such classical economists as Adam Smith (1723–1790) and David Ricardo (1772–1823). According to this theory, the value of any commodity is determined by the amount of labor put into it. This means, in effect, that workers create the values of things. Of course workers do not receive in wages what they have created in value: their wages are geared to a minimal level of subsistence. Over and above wages is surplus value, which the owners of the means of production (the bourgeoisie) appropriate as profit.

The result is that workers are exploited, for profit making takes away from workers something they create. Even worse, however, is the tendency, resulting from efforts to minimize costs and wages and to increase profits, to treat workers simply as means to profits. Workers must sell themselves, and the only relations between them and society—remembering that economic power is political power—are callous economic ones. Workers are slaves in the machinery of production. In effect, they are stripped of their humanity and, since the product of their labor is denied them and society is organized for the class interests of the bourgeoisie, workers experience greater alienation from themselves and society. There are no derived benefits of capitalism for the proletariat, for however organized the productive process, there is only anarchy in exchange. Goods and services are distributed according to money (which the proletariat does not have) rather than according to need.[7]

Behind these judgments on capitalism seem to be two chief values. The first is a version of freedom, which can be achieved when men come to understand social forces and then subject them to their own wills. The second is the principle of respect for personality, of the treatment of persons as ends rather than as means

---

[6] Another key phenomenon—though not of course limited to capitalism—is the division of labor.

[7] And in capitalism these goods are transmuted from use to commodity, which furthers exploitation and produces what Marx called commodity fetishism.

only.[8] This principle can be realized only when three conditions have been met. Private property—that is, property in the form of means to profits—must be abolished. The means of production must become communal property, so that the anarchy of capitalism will be replaced with social regulation. With the abolition of private property will come, secondly, the abolition of class distinctions. Exploitation of class by class will be impossible, men may finally become masters of their own social organization, and social *praxis* (practice and relationships) will reflect their species-being. Finally, the principle, "From each according to his ability, to each according to his needs," which is the summary statement of communist values, will be fulfilled and realized.

Marx and his followers thus propose a new society, classless and cooperative, which will be the embodiment of a new morality. Perhaps the moral principles as such are not new: indeed, Marx recognized them to be as old as the Judeo-Christian tradition. But their acceptance for social organization—their social realization— would be new; and this would mean nothing less than "the ascent of man from the kingdom of necessity to the kingdom of freedom."

Problem III: State, Power, and Authority

The communist theory of the state, power, and authority may be developed under three headings: the analysis of the state as a historical product, the use of the state in the communist revolution, and the disappearance of the state in the classless society. The first of these was developed by Engels.[9] The state, Engels insisted,

---

[8] This principle suggests the Kantian imperative introduced above under idealism. Many critics of Marx have argued, however, that the full *ethical* meaning of the principle cannot be read into Marx. If an individual reflects capitalist values and position, he is not only not to be "respected," he is an enemy to be destroyed.

[9] See his *The Origin of the Family, Private Property and the State*. Engels used materials by Marx in this work.

is not an institution forced on society from the outside, nor is it in Hegelian fashion the ultimate realization of the ethical ideal. It is a product of historical evolution, where it arises at a certain stage in the dialectical development of society, and where it will—when conditions are right—eventually disappear.

What is the stage of the state? Primarily it is when society divides itself into classes (understood in the technical sense), so that men become divided in their activities and interests. As has been seen, communists believe that the existence of classes leads inevitably to class conflicts, with one class becoming dominant and the exploiter of other classes. There is tension and resistance between classes, and consequently there is also need for some coercive power to control and keep down class conflicts. Just how any particular state is organized depends on the way its society is organized, but all states have the same function, namely to keep social peace. Yet the peace is kept in a special way: economic power is political power, which means that the class having control of economic matters also controls the state. This means in turn that the state becomes the agent of the dominant class, securing its interests at the expense and sacrifice of the interests of other classes. In brief, the state is a coercive power serving the purposes of exploitation.

The state does not exist for all eternity: it will in time be taken over and used to bring about its own destruction. This is the second communist teaching on the state, namely the dictatorship of the proletariat. Given that the state is the organization of force in society maintaining the interests of exploiters, it follows that any revolutionary class bent on changing the social order must turn the power of the state to its own purposes. Force must be used to suppress the exploiters, and such use will be exercised by the proletariat. Interestingly, communism teaches that the revolutionary class is the oppressed: it is they rather than the oppressor who make progress, for they are enlightened and disciplined by work. Establishing its own dictatorship for this purpose, the proletariat will crush the bourgeoisie and lead the masses to socialism.[10]

[10] Communism, it may be noted, is one type of socialism. It agrees with other socialist theories in such aims as the abolition of private property, but differs from them on the means of social change. Most other forms of socialism

Nearly all communist literature contains the third teaching on the state, namely its disappearance in the classless society. Summarizing his work in a letter written in 1852, Marx emphasized the traditional nature of the dictatorship of the proletariat:

> *What I did that was new was to prove: (1) that the* existence of classes *is only bound up with* particular, historic phases in the development of production; *(2) that the class struggle necessarily leads to the* dictatorship of the proletariat; *(3) that this dictatorship itself only constitutes the transition to the* abolition of all classes *and to a* classless society.

Having defined the state as organized force serving exploitation, Marx was led further to hold that in the classless society the state will disappear. There will be no class interests that political power must maintain, for private property—the property used for profit —will be eliminated. There will not be a need for force because there will no longer be alienation, which is the basic cause of crime and antisocial behavior. To be sure, Marx believed (with other socialists such as the Saint-Simonians) that there will still be the need for "administration," understood as business management and the arbitration of disputes.[11] Since, however, men and society no longer are divided and antithetical (since society conforms to men's capacities), force is unnecessary for the acceptance of management and arbitration. The social good supports, indeed is, the individual good, which is another way of observing that the classless society is the realm of freedom.

PROBLEM IV: LAW AND RIGHTS

Two ideas—both of which have been met in preceding sections —are basic for understanding the communist approach to law. The

reject communist ideas of violent revolution and the dictatorship of the proletariat.

[11] Marxism thus rejects anarchism, against which Engels wrote an article, "On Authority," in which he urged that revolution itself is "the most authoritarian thing there is."

first is economic determinism, which teaches that the level of economic development is decisive for the form of any society and its culture. "The sum total of these relations of production," said Marx, "constitutes the economic structure of society—the real foundation, on which rise legal and political superstructures and to which correspond definite forms of social consciousness." Thus belonging to the "superstructure," law, with morality, manners, and religion, is never independent of the economic substructure of society; it is always effect, never cause.[12]

The second idea is that the whole conception of law is linked with the state. This is true both of private law, which aims at individual security, and of public law, which controls utility. In all forms, law is analyzed by communists exclusively as a means of control serving class interests. More precisely, property relations (to which law is ultimately reduced) are the legal expression of relations of production, and the function of law is to maintain that class structure of society which enables some classes to exploit others.[13] But this idea must be pursued with reference to the theory of economic and historical development, for as the state is destined to wither away, so too is law. During the dictatorship of the proletariat, there is need for a "revolutionary legality," which is the coercive power to suppress opponents. Then will follow a development when, as Marx said, the narrow horizon of bourgeois law will be fully crossed and when the principle, "From each according to his ability, to each according to his needs," will be a social reality. At this point, there will be an identity of law and revolutionary consciousness such that there will be no need for the sanctions of law.

In general, it must be said that these statements about law are largely passive, for little basis is provided by them for the construction of an affirmative philosophy of law. Later communists have however recognized this, with the result that there has been a

[12] In a letter to Joseph Bloch (1890), Engels admitted that elements in the superstructure can influence historical struggles, but only regarding their *form*.

[13] As Engels put it, if the state reflects economic conditions, so does the law. This dependence is often forgotten, however, so that the superstructure is pursued for its own sake. The result is professionalism and formalism in legal practice.

development in law beyond the views found in classic sources. Engels himself came to admit that he and Marx had overstated the extent to which economic causes could be found for political and legal institutions. This seems to be an admission that, to some extent at least, law is an independent domain with principles of its own. Also, with the recognition of the need for administrative procedures in a socialist society, further modification of Marx's views becomes necessary. Later communist philosophers have therefore addressed themselves to this need to create a legal norm fully adequate to all the trends of social development.

Problem V: Political Obligation

Why is a citizen obliged to obey the state or society of which he is a member? For the communist, this question is in the end meaningless—or at least unnecessary. The reason is that a society conformable to man's nature, a society that has overcome alienation and exploitation, will be willingly obeyed. No chasm would exist between individual and society, and social life would be seen by individuals as the fulfillment, or condition of the fulfillment, of their own inner being. But this, of course, is the communist ideal. In capitalist societies, the situation is very different: citizens, especially proletarians, obey out of force and fear, not out of a sense of moral duty. The important element in the problem of political obligation is not, therefore, some theoretical answer, but rather the development of a practical program by which the ideal may be attained. Some of the details of that program can be found in the writings of Lenin.

Supple leader of the October Revolution, Lenin adopted Marx's teaching to the Russian situation, yet at the same time he always appeared "orthodox." [14] The clue to his revision of Marx

---

[14] Though a theoretical difference appeared among Russian leaders over the issue of national or world wide revolution. Leon Trotsky (1887–1940) opposed Lenin and, later, Joseph Stalin. See Trotsky's *The Defense of Terrorism*, New

is his theory of the party and of party organization. Such a theory is needed, Lenin taught, if a social class is to act as a group, and especially if a class is to be revolutionary. The development of class consciousness, which occurs when a class learns what its interests are, is primarily the result of party activity. Lenin also sought to bring the "dictatorship of the proletariat" in its Russian form into communist theory. In making communism even more explicitly a theory of social revolution, he accepted the idea that the "new state" produced by the revolution is itself an instrument of power. In effect, therefore, he came to understand the dictatorship of the proletariat as the dictatorship of the party, emphasizing therewith the notion of a conspiratorial underground movement and giving Russian communism its political character.

These ideas received expression in Lenin's first theoretical work, *What Is to Be Done?* In it, Lenin insisted that the masses must be trained for their revolutionary activity by complete political exposure, that is, by becoming self-conscious of their interests as a distinct social class. The political consciousness they achieve by this exposure comes from without rather than from within, and its source is a disciplined party organization that is the "vanguard of the revolutionary forces in our time." For Lenin communism is a dogma eliciting loyalty and serving as a scientific guide to action. When the work of the party is completed and the classless society achieved, the problem of political obligation will be resolved.

Problem VI: The Ideal of Justice

In general, ideals of justice are derived from political theories, and this is true of communism too. At the center of the theoretical apparatus of the position is a call to social justice: communism

---

York, 1921. Another interpretation of revolution—and *praxis*—was developed for the Chinese situation by Mao Tse-tung. Some of his writings are conveniently anthologized in *Mao Tse-tung: An Anthology of his Writings*, ed. Anne Fremantle, New York, 1954.

demands as well as rests on an ideal of justice that would eliminate the causes of social inequality by abolishing private ownership of the means of production. Whether discussing dialectical materialism, exploitation, classes, or alienation, Marx and his important followers were moved by the conviction that injustice can be overcome, and that, with the proper understanding of himself and society, man can establish a society that will make injustice impossible.

The principle supporting this ideal of justice has been met before: "From each according to his abilities, to each according to his needs." In turn, this principle reflects an even more fundamental ethical assumption, namely respect for personality. Marx was convinced, on the one hand, that capitalist society violates this principle. His attacks on the effects of capitalism—its resolving of personal worth into exchange value—are a documentation of this. On the other hand, he sought to formulate a social vision and the means to realize it that would maintain the conditions for the exercise of human capacities as he understood them. His conception of justice may thus be said to be a social expression (one of them, since other expressions are possible) of the ethical principle of respect for personality.

Marx believed that history is inevitably moving toward this ideal. No other outcome of the class struggle is possible. And yet he also was an activist who believed that men must strive and work to achieve justice. Communism is thus a call to action, guided, communists believe, by accurate, scientific knowledge of the laws of historical evolution. The movement of history is toward world communism, which will eliminate exploitation through the abolition of private property. The means to this goal is the dictatorship of the proletariat, which will use power not as an end in itself but to overcome class divisions altogether. The outcome of this period of social reorganization will lead to the achievement of true (rather than bourgeois) justice, and will fulfill human needs in a way fully consistent with man's species-being. In this realm of freedom with its release of human powers, culture will flourish, and an "all-conquering scientific knowledge" will guide men to their true destiny of self-fulfillment.

Bibliographical Essay

A great number of studies and anthologies—usually with introductory essays—have been published on communist thought. Among them are: Max Beer, *The Life and Teaching of Karl Marx*, London, 1925; Sidney Hook, *Towards the Understanding of Karl Marx*, New York, 1933, as well as other works; Emile Burns (ed.), *A Handbook of Marxism*, New York, 1935; Isaiah Berlin, *Karl Marx*, 2d ed., London, 1948; Jacques Barzun, *Darwin, Marx, Wagner*, Boston, 1941; R. N. C. Hunt, *The Theory and Practice of Communism*, New York, 1950; G. D. H. Cole, *A History of Socialist Thought*, 4 vols., New York, 1953–1958; Herbert Marcuse, *Soviet Marxism: A Critical Analysis*, New York, 1958; Raymond Polin, *Marxian Foundations of Communism*, Chicago, 1966; Shlomo Avineri, *The Social and Political Thought of Karl Marx*, Cambridge, 1968; and many works by Maurice Cornforth.

The basic exposition of the communist position must refer to the writings of Marx, Engels, and Lenin, but there is continuing development of communist thought, from Stalin on and in many countries. A number of anthologies on all these materials have appeared, one of the most thorough and accessible being Robert C. Tucker's *The Marx-Engels Reader*, New York, 1972, 1977. Tucker has also written scholarly monographs on communist thought. An interesting development in Marxist scholarship in the last three decades has been the emphasis on the early, "humanistic" writings of Marx. Important in this development have been such thinkers as J. Habermas, George Lukács, Herbert Marcuse, and Jean-Paul Sartre (who will be discussed in Chapter VIII). Also valuable is John Plamenatz, *Karl Marx's Philosophy of Man*, Oxford, 1975. Another significant development is the appearance in English of writings from authors in major communist nations other than Russia. A bibliography of soviet philosophy, now in five volumes, is edited by J. M. Bochenski and published by D. Reidel

Publishing Co. Many of the books listed above touch on later developments, and a number of journals reprint important Russian and communist philosophical papers in English, including *Science and Society, Praexis,* and *Soviet Studies in Philosophy.*

CHAPTER 7

Pragmatism

Pragmatism is America's most distinctive contribution to the world community of philosophy. Developed partly in interaction with the American experience, partly in relation to the continually maturing science of the nineteenth century, and especially influenced by the theory of evolution, it became a many-sided movement that affected much of American culture, including law, education, and political thought. Its chief philosophic spokesmen were Charles Sanders Peirce (1839–1914), William James (1842–1910), and John Dewey (1859–1952), though lesser known philosophers like Chauncey Wright (1830–1875) and lawyers like Nicholas St. John Green (1835–1876) and Oliver Wendell Holmes, Jr. (1841–1935), contributed to the movement and helped to bring the pragmatic spirit into many areas of intellectual concern.

What is pragmatism? Writing for the *Century Dictionary* in 1909, Dewey gave the following as the basic meaning of the term amid all its uses: "The theory that the processes and the materials of knowledge are determined by practical or purposive considerations—that there is no such thing as knowledge determined by exclusively theoretical, speculative, or abstract intellectual considerations." Two years earlier, James published an essay on "What Pragmatism Means" [1] in which he asserted in a similar vein that any purely objective truth, that is, any truth supposedly established apart from the function of giving human satisfaction, is nowhere

[1] Lecture II in *Pragmatism, A New Name for Some Old Ways of Thinking*, New York, 1907.

121

to be found. To illustrate this point (and others), James began his article with an anecdote about a "metaphysical" problem. Imagine a squirrel clinging to one side of a tree and a human witness standing on the opposite side. The witness tries to sight the squirrel by moving around the tree, but the squirrel moves fast enough in the opposite direction that it is never seen. Now the man goes around the tree and the squirrel is on the tree. The vexing question is, does the man go around the squirrel? To take sides on this question, however, is to begin an interminable dispute unless one condition is met, namely to decide what is *practically meant* by "going around" the squirrel. If one's meaning is to occupy positions of east, north, west, and south of the squirrel, the man does go around it; if one means to stand in front, then to the side, and then to the rear of the squirrel, he does not go around the squirrel. With this distinction made, there is no longer really any dispute: "You are both right and both wrong according as you conceive the verb 'to go round' on one practical fashion or the other."

This illustration suggests that pragmatism is both a theory of meaning and knowledge and a revolt against certain speculative, abstract philosophies. The key notions for these sides of pragmatism are "purpose in thought" and "practical consequences." Before analyzing their meaning more carefully, however, it may be helpful to look first at two of the influences on pragmatism mentioned above, namely the theory of evolution and experimental science. Writing of evolutionary theory, Dewey said that "the influence of Darwin upon philosophy resides in his having conquered the phenomena of life for the principle of transition, and thereby freed the new logic for application to mind, life, and morals." [2] Three ideas are contained in this quotation. Having conquered the phenomena of life, Darwin showed, first, that nature includes man and intelligence. No supernatural or extranatural principle is needed to account for man or his capacities: they are products of the evolutionary process itself. Secondly, Darwin suggested the priority of transition over permanence, of becoming over

2 "The Influence of Darwin on Philosophy," *The Influence of Darwin on Philosophy and Other Essays in Contemporary Thought*, New York, 1910. This whole essay is important for details on Darwin's influence on pragmatism.

being. No fixed species, no eternal forms, are necessary or warranted. Thirdly, therefore, intelligence itself is naturalized. The function of thought can no longer be to conceive eternal principles or natural laws. It cannot "look back" to grasp fixed structures. Mind attempts to control events by looking forward to consequences in order to secure those conditions that will best serve human purposes. A new logic will stress methods for such control rather than so-called timeless laws of thought.

These same interpretations, pragmatists believe, are given support by the practices of experimental science. In the "laboratory method," as Peirce called it, ideas are basically hypotheses or proposed solutions to felt problems. Hypotheses predict consequences, and methods of verification are pursued by scientists to determine which consequences can be found in experience and which hypotheses, therefore, are confirmed. Experimental thinking is related to doing in terms of purpose, for it involves the manipulation of present means according to conceived consequences for the purpose of subsequent control.

As a philosophic revolt, then, pragmatism is a movement that rejects philosophies which speculate on abstractions or empty first principles. It looks to concrete cases, to particular consequences, and to ideas and meanings that will "make a difference." It is also against monistic and absolutistic positions: there are no "wholesale views" of reality (Dewey) or single solutions for the problems of men. Pragmatists also reject purely logical procedures such as coherence as a method of thought for either facts or values. Thought is experimental, and its full meaning includes active manipulation and control beyond logical inference.

Positively, pragmatists developed a new theory of knowledge and truth. An idea is a plan of action, a hypothesis to be tested, an instrument [3] whose function is to guide inquiries to the satisfactory resolution of problematic situations. Thinking is best understood as response to the doubtful, and knowledge "is the fruit of the undertakings that transform a problematic situation into a resolved one" (Dewey). True hypotheses or beliefs are those which

---

[3] Dewey often used the term instrumentalism because of this understanding of the function of ideas.

lead to the successful resolution of problems, and the test of whether a belief is true is whether acting upon it leads to practical consequences which are satisfying.

Thus the true is "that which works," that which is successful in solving problems. Properly understood, this brief statement provides a convenient summary of pragmatic epistemology. But it also raises one more introductory matter that must be treated, for pragmatists have differed somewhat in their views about what practical consequences are to be considered satisfactory. These differences also provide a convenient basis for distinguishing the main varieties of pragmatism. To the question, then, of what satisfactory consequence is the test of truth, there is the answer of *humanistic* pragmatism: that which fulfills human purposes and desires is true. In some of his writings, particularly on ethics and religion, James took this position, as did the English pragmatist, F. C. S. Schiller (1864–1937). A second answer is *experimental*: truth is what works in the sense of the experimentally verified. A subform of experimentalism is *nominalistic* pragmatism. The results of ideas are expected in the form of particular perceptual facts in future experiences. The meaning of, and true statements about, human nature, for example, are not about some essence "Man," but are rather about the particular doings of particular men. Peirce and James (in his "tough-minded" writings) took an experimental, and occasionally nominalistic, position. Finally, there is the *biological* version of pragmatism associated with Dewey. Thought is purposive in seeking to help the organism adapt to its environment, and successful adaptation in terms of survival and growth provides the criterion for the truth of ideas.

In its emphasis on science and experimental method, pragmatism has something in common with positivism, and its stress on consequences links it with utilitarianism. Despite this indebtedness, however, it differs from them both: from positivism because of its concern with an experimentalist approach to values,[4] and from utilitarianism because of its evolutionary and instrumentalist view of mind and its interest in all shared values rather than pleasures alone. Thus, while its relations with earlier theories may

---

[4] This matter is treated below in the section on "Social and Political Values."

easily be traced, pragmatism constitutes a distinctive philosophic perspective.

PROBLEM I: MAN AND SOCIETY

The pragmatist's attention to consequences and their control through intelligence is the basis of his understanding of man and society: he appeals neither to special forces outside the course of observable phenomena nor to fictional devices or special causes to account for man's social behavior. Man is a social animal, for association rather than isolation is a law of everything that exists; he becomes a social animal because the content of his developing experience is itself social. The question, therefore, of how individuals come to be associated in their various groups is hardly a proper question at all.

Yet the question of how social connections develop in the ways they do is a proper question, and it arises because individuals are led in terms of their interests to think of the consequences of their behavior on themselves and others. These consequences become matters of observation and possible control, and therewith they take on new possibilities for value through relation to intelligence. Interest in the consequences of associative life turns to such matters as survival, habits of action, and thought as well as choice in terms of consequences. These ends are served by numerous social groups, each of which is formed when shared interests are felt and consequences are appreciated.

Thus, society is to be viewed, not as an entity in itself, but as a collection of interacting "primary groups." Many of these groups, however, have consequences on persons other than those who participate in them. Hence there arises a distinct, though secondary, interest in public forms of associative life including the state. To these forms belongs the supervision of the consequences of primary groups, which do not themselves go beyond their own shared interests.

This pragmatic understanding of man and society is stated in terms of inquiry or man as a problem solver, puralism of groups, interests, and consequences.[5] Underlying these notions is the belief that associated action is a universal trait of existence. Such action has results, and some results of human action are perceived or noted. Then come purposes and plans to secure those consequences that are desired. Since some interests concern only the group while others have broader consequences, a common interest is also generated. Hence arises the "public," whose interest is directed toward the control of these broader consequences.

PROBLEM II: SOCIAL AND POLITICAL VALUES

Rejecting eternal truths and fixed patterns in the study of fact, pragmatists similarly deny that value can be understood by reference to ready-made and over-all patterns or objective structures. Value and disvalue are qualities of interest and desire that arise within the context of human experience, attaching themselves to the consequences of courses of action. Further, the problem of value relates to that control of experience which will establish values, not to merely theoretical manipulation of general concepts.

Dewey's efforts to develop a logic of valuation have had a wide influence.[6] Like all inquiries, valuation begins with the recognition of a problematic situation—in this case, a conflict in desires. Using knowledge gained in previous inquiries, one sets up a hypothesis or proposed solution to the conflict that serves as an end-in-view. The end-in-view guides subsequent actions that create the objective conditions and control the consequences through which a value is instituted and the original conflict resolved. The movement is thus from the desired to the desirable; the method followed is the tentative, experimental method of intelligence; and

[5] Dewey wrote of social issues in many works; on association see especially *The Public and Its Problems*, New York, 1927.

[6] See his brief statement in *Theory of Valuation*, Chicago, 1939.

—as is true of pragmatism generally—the direction of control is toward consequences.

In his discussions of social values, Dewey rejected conceptions of individual and society that are based on a logic of general concepts.[7] The need is for concrete guidance and inquiry. Social arrangements, Dewey said, must not be viewed as means to progress or as the guarantee of happiness: they are means for creating individuals. So understood, these arrangements become the object of detailed inquiry about how to release and strengthen human capacities. The release of capacities, however, is possible only through communication, sharing, and joint participation in society's goods. Thus, the general problem of social and political values is the institution of those social conditions whose consequences insure the joint participation of persons in shared experiences. The growth of persons through such participation, Dewey concluded, gives freedom its meaning, and conjoint and communicated experience is the defining phrase for democracy.

A second pragmatic approach to value was developed by William James, who began with the assertion that value is not some principle rooted in antecedent being, but is consequent upon human feelings and desires.[8] Sentient life is the "habitat of value," and apart from persons, terms like good and bad have no meaning or application. That is, the universe itself—or anything else— cannot be considered good or bad except in relation to desires. But, said James, one other condition is needed for the existence of an ethical world, and this is the requirement of many persons. Given a pluralism of desiring beings, there arises the conflict of interests and ideals, as well as the claims of individuals to fulfill their desires and to oblige others to respect their fulfillment.

Thus there are opposing claims and values and it must be decided how to choose among them. Not, James insisted, "by any abstract moral 'nature of things' existing antecedently to the concrete thinkers themselves with their ideals." Any desire is imperative, and every claim produces an obligation. The rightness that is

[7] In, for example, *Reconstruction in Philosophy*, New York, 1920.

[8] "The Moral Philosopher and the Moral Life," in *The Will to Believe and Other Essays in Popular Philosophy*, New York, 1909.

sought must be concrete, a right after—and by virtue of—the fact that claims are actually made. No single abstract principle is useful, accurate, or indeed even possible. The best act is the one that makes for the "best whole" of goods, in the sense of provoking the least amount of dissatisfaction.

While both of these theories fall clearly within pragmatism, they also reflect two sides or emphases of the tradition. On the whole, James's views are more individualistic, more subjectivist, even more romantic. Pragmatists who follow James are likely to retain this same emphasis. The instrumentalism of Dewey, on the other hand, is more social, objectivist, and scientific in nature. The import of James's position is thus primarily, though not exclusively, in the area of individual choice and conduct; the stress of Dewey's is on society and culture. Dewey in fact understood philosophy to be the critic of culture, and to have a normative function. On the whole, therefore, his writings have a wider relevance to social philosophy than do James's, though the indirect influence of the latter on social discussion should not be underemphasized.

Problem III: State, Power, and Authority

Dewey's theory of man and society assigns a fundamental role to interests in associative phenomena. Rejecting attempts to understand society through abstractions like State, Law, and Sovereignty, he began with the existence of many groups resting on shared interests and pursuing desired consequences. Within this pluralistically conceived society, however, there arises a general or common interest relating to the consequences of group activity on those not participating in that activity. The state develops from this interest.

Further analysis of this pragmatic account of the state has been given by many writers, including for example the influential views of R. M. MacIver (1882–1969).[9] Having its basis in human

9 *The Modern State*, Oxford, 1926.

interests, the state is but one association among many others. Yet it is a distinctive kind of association, with a unique function of its own. That function is to give unity to the whole system of social relationships, sustaining and controlling them as well as making them possible. More simply, the state supports the "business of life," for within its unity all the different primary groups of society may find their proper place. This it does because it is given the power to dispense and guarantee rights to groups and individuals.

Such power is universal in principle: it extends over all members of a society and even to the entire human race. What is the source of this authority and power? Since the pragmatist insists that all relations and value derive from the subjective valuations of human beings, he answers this question by holding that the state is sustained by the general community as the expression of common interest. It is thus the community that gives the state its functions and powers—though the community itself is not an organization, but the source of organization.

It may be asked, how can the power that determines rights be itself limited? In two ways, MacIver answered: the state is limited by its function, and by the community that assigns to it that function. To be sure, particular states may overstep these bounds and become oppressive agents; yet they thereby lose their effectiveness as the sustainers of communities. The state is and remains a true unifying agent, MacIver concluded, only as it has evolved toward a democracy. Its character is that of a corporation, and its true nature is revealed in the fundamental meaning of law.

PROBLEM IV: LAW AND RIGHTS

Two schools of jurisprudence have developed under the influence of pragmatism. One is known as sociological jurisprudence and is associated especially with Roscoe Pound,[10] who wrote of it that

[10] The section following on "The Ideal of Justice" gives Pound's views more fully.

> *the sociological movement in jurisprudence is a movement for*
> *pragmatism as a philosophy of law; for the adjustment of princi-*
> *ples and doctrines to the human conditions they are to govern*
> *rather than to assumed first principles; for putting the human*
> *factor in the central place and relegating logic to its true position*
> *as an instrument.*[11]

This brief quotation contains or alludes to the chief elements of
the pragmatic view of law. There is the rejection of appeals to
so-called first principles, to self-evident assumptions, and to rationalistic theories of natural law. Decisions must be made with reference to their specific consequences; antecedent material such as
tradition and precedent serves as a guide for analysis, but not as a
norm for evaluation.

Rules of law are projections into the future. They attempt to
prophesy the effect on the social order of the conduct they regulate.
More broadly put, law and the courts constitute a scheme of instruments for readaptation, for assisting society in experiments of
readjustment. There is also the centrality of the human factor, of
needs and interests. Law is not logical deduction, it is a kind
of "social engineering" that aims at maximizing satisfactions and
minimizing wants. Pound summarized by writing that, "for the
purpose of understanding the law of today, I am content with a
picture of satisfying as much of the whole body of human wants
as we may with the least sacrifice."

The second school, influenced by Oliver Wendell Holmes
(1841–1935), is legal realism. Many scholars find it difficult to
distinguish sharply between realism and sociological jurisprudence:
the former seems to be a subdivision of the latter. Legal realism's
emphasis is more scientific, even positivistic—though it will be remembered that pragmatism has affinities with positivism—and it
lays greater stress on the implicit relativism of pragmatic value
theory. While accepting with sociological jurisprudence the understanding of law as prophecy as to what the courts lay down, realists

[11] Pound's interpretations of various movements in jurisprudence are given in
the first chapters of *An Introduction to the Philosophy of Law*, New Haven,
1922, 1954.

tend to limit themselves to "scientific" descriptions of the legal process, and thus also to exclude consideration of legal ideals.

One of the most influential statements of this position is Justice Holmes's "The Path of the Law." [12] In it Holmes called his reader's attention to how the rules of law actually work, not to what they may be on paper. Thus he was led to his famous definition of law as a prophecy of what the courts will do in fact. This notion applies to rights and duties also, for there is no right or duty independent of the consequences of its breach. A right, therefore, may similarly be defined as a prediction that if a man does (or does not do) a certain thing, he will suffer in certain ways by judgment of the court.

In addition to this question of definition, two other matters concerned Holmes. The first is the distinction between law and morals. Failure to make this distinction, he said, is not only conceptually confusing, but it may lead to the failure to see the nature of law as prophecy. The second is that logic is not the only force at work in law: experience is there in an even more important way. Almost any conclusion can be given logical form. The truer stuff of the law is human needs and purposes, and the goal of the law is to develop a civilized, rational system where "every rule it contains is referred articulately and definitely to an end it subserves, and when the grounds for desiring that end are stated or are ready to be stated in words."

Problem V: Political Obligation

The grounds for the pragmatist's treatment of political obligation have now been given. They include the basic associative nature of human experience, the diversity of interests, the appeal to intelligence as a means of control, and the determination of value in terms of desirable consequences. Summarizing the prag-

[12] Often reprinted, this article first appeared in the *Harvard Law Review*, 10 (1897).

matic view for many thinkers is the work of Harold J. Laski (1893–1950),[13] an English political theorist who acknowledged James as the philosophical source and inspiration of his own views. This influence is central to Laski's theory of value: "What I mean by 'right,' " he said, "is something the pragmatist will understand. It is something the individual ought to concede because experience has proved it to be good."

Laski's theory of political obligation rests on the pragmatic assumptions that the good of individuals cannot, over the long run, be separated from the goods of other men, and that intelligence is valuable as it helps to make possible the future harmony of interests. Man is a community-building animal, for his many and diverse interests are fundamentally social in nature. But in any community, private or group decisions are insufficient for the good of the whole, and spontaneity of action is impractical if not occasionally dangerous. Hence arises the necessity of government as "the final depository of the social will." The ideal for government is that the general purpose it supports will embody individual purposes, and that it will provide the means for developing human capacities. Should the mechanisms of state and society fail, human faculties remain to that degree unrealized.

Society and government are thus rooted in the complex facts of human nature. The obligation to obey arises from these same facts. Human beings develop their capacities in the shared experience of social groups, and at the same time, they are largely determined by social institutions. Men's allegiance to social institutions, however, cannot be explained in purely rational terms, for these institutions—including the state—reflect a variety of yearnings and interests. Allegiance comes as authority, and the maintenance of rules is experienced as an instrumentality for the control of desirable consequences. Realized desires, even freedom itself, rest on obedience to the common interest reflected in rules of order; the obligation to obey that order rests on the fact that it is in the individual's interest that there be a common interest.

Laski concluded with the observation that his theory is a revised Benthamism. Once again the influence of utilitarianism

---

[13] *A Grammar of Politics*, London, 1939.

on pragmatism must be noted. The pragmatic theory of political obligation rests on the general utility of society to mankind, and yet important differences between the positions remain. Pragmatists reject the hedonism of utilitarians, and insist on an instrumentalist role for intelligence in the control of consequences.

PROBLEM VI: THE IDEAL OF JUSTICE

As law is the prophecy of what the courts will do, so pragmatists assert that just law means the prophecy of what will produce the most satisfactory consequences. Justice becomes an attribute of a legal rule through its relation to subsequent experience, or put another way, every rule of law is just or unjust according to its subsequent justification. Indeed, the justice of a rule is the process of its justification, which means that the "just" is the expedient in adapting the legal order to an order of wants and interests.[14]

These general statements were developed by Roscoe Pound (1870–1964).[15] Long-time dean of the Harvard Law School, Pound exerted a great influence on American jurisprudence, not only within sociological jurisprudence, with which he was closely identified, but on legal realism and analytic jurisprudence as well. Resting his analysis on a theory of interests—"Individual interests are the only real interests"—Pound accepted the pragmatic formula that "the essence of good is to satisfy demand." He classified interests as public, social, and private, and believed that the task of law is to balance interests at the least cost by "social engineering" (another term associated with his name).

Unlike some pragmatists, Pound rejected complete relativism and skepticism, and toward the end of his long career, he favored

---

[14] See also James in "Pragmatism's Conception of Truth": "Truth *happens* to an idea. It *becomes* true, is *made* true by events." And again, " '*The true*,' *to put it very briefly, is only the expedient in the way of our thinking, just as* '*the right*' *is only the expedient in the way of our behaving.*"

[15] See the work cited above, and *Social Control through Law*, New Haven, 1942.

a definition of law that includes reference to an ideal of justice. Thus, while recognizing an ideal element,[16] Pound retained the link with individual interests and offered no definition of justice himself.

Pound of course reviewed theories of the authority of law, including those based on force, on consent, and on political ethics. Finding that the legal order keeps its authority because it harmonizes conflicting human demands and thereby maintains civilization, he rejected these theories, and instead accepted the theory of obedience to the law as motivated primarily by *habits* of obedience. To draw this conclusion is also to reject theories of the legal order based on divine or natural order, on pure reason, and on historical experience: none of these provides a measure or a standard—"justice"—that is applicable in legal experience.

How, then, does the law go about measuring value in practice? Three methods are possible: by experience, through which men learn the rules and procedures that will adjust interests and demands; by reason, by which men can formulate "jural postulates" or principles for the law as the presuppositions of civilized society; and by an ideal of legal order, against which men can judge authoritatively the value of particular rules. Pound concluded that philosophers do not agree on this ideal, and yet the law must go on. It must rely, therefore, on the first two methods, developing by reason and experience those ways of adjusting relations that, with the least waste, will give the greatest effect to the whole scheme of interests.

Bibliographical Essay

The various meanings of pragmatism were first analyzed in a classic paper by Arthur O. Lovejoy, "The Thirteen Pragmatisms," *Journal of Philosophy,* 5 (1908); it has been reprinted in many anthologies, such as Muelder, Sears, and Schlabach, *The Develop-*

---

[16] This is not necessarily inconsistent with other pragmatists, but is more a matter of emphasis. Dewey, for example, acknowledged the role of ideals in inquiry where they indicate possibilities for realization.

ment of American Philosophy, 2d ed., Boston, 1960. Good statements on pragmatism are found in this work (see Section Six) and in other books such as Herbert W. Schneider, *A History of American Philosophy*, New York, 1946; W. H. Werkmeister, *A History of Philosophical Ideas in America*, New York, 1949; Stow Persons, *American Minds: A History of Ideas*, New York, 1958; and John E. Smith, *The Spirit of American Philosophy*, New York, 1963. Especially interesting are the studies by John Dewey, "The Development of American Pragmatism," in *Studies in the History of Ideas*, New York, 1925; G. H. Mead, "The Philosophies of Royce, James, and Dewey in Their American Setting," *Ethics*, 40 (1929); and Philip P. Wiener, *Evolution and the Founders of Pragmatism*, Cambridge, Mass., 1949.

A general though critical treatment of pragmatic social philosophy is found in W. Y. Elliott, *The Pragmatic Revolt in Politics*, New York, 1928. Many shorter studies may be found in philosophical journals. Two other books touching on pragmatism in this area may be mentioned: Morton White, *Social Thought in America: The Revolt Against Formalism*, New York, 1949; and Richard Hofstadter, *Social Darwinism in American Thought, 1860–1915*, rev. ed., Boston, 1955. A recent work which includes an exposition of pragmatism as well as an evaluation of the movement in relation to other social philosophies is Richard J. Bernstein's *Praxis and Action*, Philadelphia, 1971.

Existentialism

Widely read and discussed, existentialism is viewed by many as an expression of the moods and experiences of twentieth-century man. To a large extent, it is a protest. It speaks out against various forms of dehumanization that it believes result from industrial technology, nationalism, militarism, and scientific "objectivism." Modern mass society, existentialists find, leads to alienation, to self-deception, and to the denial of nobility. Modern man's penchant for systematization—in science, in philosophy, in social theory—issues in the loss of subjectivity. Events and tendencies such as these mean that human values are in a state of crisis, and that human freedom is threatened with extinction.

What is existentialism? When used broadly, the term refers to a type of thinking that emphasizes human existence and the qualities peculiar to it rather than to nature or the physical world. Man-centered and individualistic, existentialism seeks to probe the often darker corners of the human situation. Yet "emphasis on human existence," though the beginning of a definition, is actually too vague for use in reference to this contemporary philosophy. Many, if not most, philosophers of the past have also been concerned about the human condition, and religion addresses itself to human life as well.

The existentialist's attention to man grows out of specifically modern conditions and concludes in unique insights. As suggested above, these conditions include the loss of the individual in mass culture and technology, the consequent alienation of the human person from himself as well as from his productions, and the evaporation of meaning in life through divisions within the human spirit. The response of persons to them is frequently called the "existentialist experience." Recorded by many artists and writers as well as by philosophers, it is a sense of the decomposition of man's experienced world—first, of all rational concepts and systems, next of stable objects, then of time and history, until finally all coherence, meaning, and value are gone—to the point where one faces only the Nothing and experiences only despair. Together with the description of this decomposition, existentialists analyze men's anxieties in such boundary or "limit" situations as guilt and death. This experience, sometimes also called an experience of crisis, has arisen in times of social and personal catastrophe in the twentieth century.

Existentialism is not simply a philosophy of despair and crisis, whatever conditions produce it. A second expression, "the existentialist attitude," indicates that reflection on the existentialist experience can result in an important philosophical position. This attitude is also directed toward human existence. Other philosophers study man, but they view him in terms of some systematic concept or essence derived from reason. Existentialists oppose such traditional conceptualism and its abstract, general concepts of existence and individuality. Neither systems of thought nor rational definitions can capture individual human existence. Man must be understood, existentialists insist, in terms of possibilities, anxieties, and decisions; in terms of the tragic and absurd situations in which he finds himself. Man is not an image or reflection of an antecedently existing essence that determines his actions and his values; he is a free being. *What* man is can only be inferred from *how* he is, that is, man's essence is to be found only in his concrete existence. The desire to know the meaning of the individual man in a more radical way than have other philosophers leads existentialists to hold that the starting point of philosophy is the concrete situation of man in the world.

Much of existentialist writing aims to describe the whole of human life—not just reason but emotional and conative states as well. Reason and rational structure are not equivalent to human life: feeling, passion, and decision are equally if not more important

clues to man's being. Yet existentialism is more than phenomenology, great as is its reliance on descriptive techniques. It also
seeks to know the reality of human existence and, for some existentialists, to produce a theory of being. The phenomenological
interest is directed toward an ontological goal, though the latter
can be achieved only through the former.

This ontological interest links existentialism with certain aspects of traditional philosophy, though it would agree to some
extent with positivism and other antimetaphysical positions in
their distrust of philosophic rationalism. Existentialism, in turn,
has questions about these latter philosophies and, in particular,
takes issue with efforts to make philosophy another technology. It
doubts that science or reason can interpret the whole universe, and
it is suspicious of the "disinterestedness" of modern objective
thought. Its closer tie is with realism and idealism although, as
has been suggested in these paragraphs, its approach to human
existence is unique.

It is difficult to go beyond these introductory generalizations
in describing existentialism. Writing of individuality as a constant
theme, existentialists are themselves fervidly individual: they refuse
to belong to schools and systems and, for the most part, they do
not offer doctrines in the traditional sense. Indeed, they more often
speak of philosophizing than philosophy, for their message is as
much a call to self-examination and decision as the giving of
new information. Some existentialists such as Jean-Paul Sartre
(1905–   ) have produced atheistic versions of existentialism;
others like Karl Jaspers (1883–1969) and Gabriel Marcel (1887–
1973) have produced theistic versions (the former nondenomina-
tional, the latter Roman Catholic); and yet others have followed
Martin Heidegger (1889–1976), who has left the religious question
open. Even the use of the term existentialist is disputed, some of
these men accepting it, others rejecting it.

Because of these observations, it might be more accurate to
say that this chapter attempts to develop certain existentialist ideas
rather than existentialism as a single position. There is much debate
in the literature as to who are and who are not existentialists, and
as just indicated, some of the men usually called existentialists have

themselves rejected the label. Little mention, therefore, is made in the following materials of the problem of proper classification (though it is recognized that, while Jaspers would ordinarily be placed in the position, Niebuhr ordinarily would not); instead, attention is given to the social implications of existentialist themes.

The individuality and uniqueness of existentialists are carried over into their social philosophy. No "system" of government and society is given: existentialists are more interested in man than in government, in how man feels about law and society than in what these are in themselves. As a protest movement, existentialism provides more criticism than construction. Yet, here too, certain themes are identifiable. In general, stable social forms and processes are desirable, but often men tend to divide the ends sought from the means taken to realize them. There is, so to speak, an alienation of means and ends, with a consequent loss of ends and a brutalization of means. There is little agreement among existentialists on the meaning of social ends: Pascal accepted the absolute monarchy under which he was born, for he saw nothing better; Sartre has embraced a version of Marxism; Kierkegaard was suspicious of democracy; and Nietzsche seems at times to have been almost an anarchist. But existentialists have agreed that only disaster can result if trust is placed in social organizations and ideologies for the wrong reasons. Such trust may lead to a failure to take "risks" against abuses, it may involve a retreat from freedom, and it may issue in destructive idolization of power and organization.

Existentialism thus entails no specific political program—perhaps even no social philosophy—in the sense that other philosophies produce them.[1] With Pascal, most existentialists view society and government as objects of neither esteem nor contempt. They claim these contribute little or nothing to man's perfection, though they can be sources of degradation and therefore must be carefully watched. Not systematic social philosophy, existentialist writings nevertheless provide important source materials for the student of society.

---

[1] Although Sartre is close to being an exception to this statement in his later writings, and some philosophers have found in Heidegger the premises, at least, of a social philosophy. Amplification of these observations is given below.

PROBLEM I: MAN AND SOCIETY

The individuality and diversity of existentialist thinkers make generalization about them difficult on this problem as well as on all others in this chapter. The concern for subjectivity and the human condition just written about is one common theme, although the particular ontologies of human nature developed by existentialists have varied widely; and a sense of distrust, even of negativity, of social organization is something of a second theme. But it is perhaps better to illustrate than to generalize, and for this purpose an older and a contemporary existentialist have been selected.

Although the number of thinkers before the nineteenth and twentieth centuries who reflect the existentialist position is small, one—the French mathematician and philosopher Blaise Pascal (1623–1662)—surely belongs within the stream of existentialism.[2] Caught in the religious strife of his day and yet also a contributor to the rising science of the seventeenth century, he was a sensitive observer of the human condition with its frailty, uncertainty, and despair.

Pascal was well aware of man's need to feel at home in the world. But as man looks at himself in relation to the world, he is caught between Nothing and the Infinite, a something yet not everything. Still, he has looked, and perhaps also has aspired to everything, though the only result is a sense of his own insignificance. This awareness of insignificance points to man as a being with reason, for man looks for what only a thinking being can seek—and he sees only misery. Pascal taught that man's sense of insignificance comes paradoxically from what is most excellent in him, namely reason.

Reason, moreover, is an even more basic source of human wretchedness: not only can man think, but he can think about

[2] See his *Thoughts*, tr. W. F. Trotter, New York, 1910, and other editions.

himself. He is thus led to make himself the center of everything, becoming irksome to others because of his wish to enslave them. Each self is the enemy of all other selves and aspires to tyranny over them; in his self-centeredness man spends his life concerned about some "image" of himself in the minds of others. In fact, he is concerned about this image to himself. Unable to face himself as he is, he masks his true motives and lives in the untruth of self-deception. Once again, man's highest excellence, reason, becomes the source of his deepest misery, for the triviality of man comes from his fear of truth. To escape this wretched condition, man must learn to see himself as he really is. The pursuit of this truth—of what is high and what is base in man—leads ultimately to God. Before man finds God, however, he is afflicted by vanity and by the need to escape from himself, and this is the condition for which social order and government are the remedies.

Like Hobbes, Pascal taught that men are enemies of each other and that government is a curb on passion and pride (though his assumptions differ radically from those of Hobbes). Indeed, men are also enemies of themselves, and only divine grace can save them from the consequences of this. The basis of society is thus might and necessity. Pascal posited no ideal of justice for society and he remained as skeptical about reason as Hume: if there is a real or essential justice, it eludes man. He was also indifferent to questions of political obligation and the legitimacy of government. The legal order adds nothing to man's perfection; perfection must be found in man's spiritual dimension.

Pascal's writings touch on many of the recurring themes of existentialist thought: the problem of knowing oneself, the distrust of science and reason for existential concerns, the uncertainties of existence, the nothingness of man's being, the elusiveness of finality, the reality of temporality and change, and man's corruption—his untruth—as revealed in disguise, falsehood, and hypocrisy. Many of them will be met again in subsequent sections.

A second existentialist view having wide influence is found in the work of Sartre. In his earlier masterpiece, *Being and Nothing* (English translation, 1956) he developed the radical hypothesis that man is subjectivity and freedom—terms which in the end have the same meaning—or, as he was to put it in a popular lecture,[3] that for man existence precedes essence. To hold this doctrine means that man first appears, and only later defines himself in his experience. Since there is no antecedent essence to which he must conform, man is both free and responsible for the definition he produces. Sartre thus grounds his entire ontology in human choice, which itself has no ground: in his freedom man exists outside and beyond himself or his essence, and this in fact is existence. *Being and Nothing* is a lengthy exploration of the meaning and implications of this radical freedom in the various dimensions of human experience.

Although *Being and Nothing* did not overlook the social dimension of man's existence, Sartre's influence in social philosophy has only really developed as he has attempted to produce a Marxist version of existentialism.[4] Although his commitment to freedom remains in this later work—and sometimes puts him at odds with Marx's historical materialism for its implicit determinism [5]—Sartre believes there are sufficient intellectual sources in Marx to link his theories to them.

Man, Sartre now says, is a being of needs—for food, companionship, security, and so on. But scarcity, a cornerstone phenomenon for Sartre, governs the human condition, two consequences of which are the experience of alienation and the perception of the Other as a threat. Man must of course labor to satisfy his needs, even in the presence of the Other, and Sartre traces social development from man's powerless position in an unorganized seriality through gropings toward group structures to solidification into an organization—where man is still powerless—under institutions. All this, so to speak, happens: human beings become caught in the restrictions

---

[3] "Existentialism," in *Existentialism and Human Emotions*, tr. Bernard Frechtman, New York, 1957.

[4] Or an existentialist version of Marxism: interpreters disagree. Sartre's most important books in this effort are *A Question of Method*, English tr., New York, 1973, and *Critique of Dialectical Reason*, English tr., Atlantic Highlands, N.J., 1976.

[5] Sartre attacks Soviet Marxism for "burying the Subject."

and passivities of social life which Sartre calls the Practico-Inert. Daily life is hell, and man is a "useless passion." [6]

Such limitations on man's freedom become the objects of Sartre's attack—and he may in fact have adopted Marxism in the face of an offensive bourgeoise society. But in his *praxis*, man can, despite these seeming limitations, discover that he is more than an object (for Sartre a fundamental mistake in Marx who held that in capitalist labor, man becomes an object). He can then understand his being as being-outside-himself, and realize that his real being is still to be found in freedom and consciousness. Nevertheless, Sartre concludes that the Marxist vision of society promises the least threatening and restricting of social alternatives because it calls for the destruction of capitalist power relations.

PROBLEM II: SOCIAL AND POLITICAL VALUES

While Pascal's writings are an important anticipation of existentialism, the real origin of the movement is with another thinker, Soren Kierkegaard (1813–1855), although mention must be made again of the difficulty of classification, for it has been debated whether Kierkegaard was in fact an existentialist. Kierkegaard's central theme is how one may become a Christian—he was essentially a religious author—and much of his writing defends Christianity against false values. His own age, he believed, had forgotten what it means to be a Christian, or even what it means *to be*. Hence he was led, many say for the first time, to introduce into Western thought the categories of "existence" and "individual."

By existence, Kierkegaard means the striving of a person to fulfill himself at the highest level of development. Concrete and individual, existence is also unique, irreducible, and not concep-

---

[6] Sartre here seems to be accepting the Marxist principle that the mode of production dominates the development of social life.

tualizable: more technically, it is possibility. Since men must strive and decide in relation to the possible, their lives point to a tension within their very being. In describing and analyzing various experiences such as dread and despair, Kierkegaard found this tension to be a result of the fact that man is a synthesis of the temporal and eternal, of the finite and infinite—in short, that man is a spiritual being.

Ultimately, for Kierkegaard, existence means to stand "before God." To exist simply as a synthesis is not yet to be a spiritual being, for meaning and purpose have not been achieved. True selfhood can be reached only when the self is related to the Power that constitutes the synthesis (even though men may try to find substitutes for God in pleasure, duty, or some totalitarian political program). Only decision or faith can bring meaning into the individual human life, and the achievement of meaning is "subjective truth."

Kierkegaard's writings [7] on political and social values are mainly critical, for his concern in this area was with the convergence of movements in the century against the individual. In brief, Kierkegaard believed that his age was witnessing an abdication of selfhood: democracy was trusting the crowd, the power of reason, and the spread of progress. But the multitude is an absurd monster: "the crowd, regarded as a judge over ethical and religious matters, is untruth." Reason seeks man-made absolutes—which means no absolutes—so that the whole of existence sinks into "average behavior" without passion or individual existence. The "progress" of the age is science and technology, which are but tools that will only hasten the loss of the individual in urban and industrial masses. Reason and progress lead to secularism, the "levelling process," "faceless multitudes," and therewith the deification of state or society. Kierkegaard, in fact, described secular social movements such as socialism and communism as religions of salvation, though idolatrous ones because they assume that society is everything. As one critic has put it, "Kierkegaard understood better than anyone and before anyone the creative diabolical

---

[7] Many passages are relevant. See especially *The Present Age*, tr. Alexander Dru, New York, 1962.

principle of the mass: fleeing from one's own person, no longer being responsible, and therefore no longer guilty, and becoming at one stroke a participant in the divinized power of the Anonymous." [8]

Kierkegaard described the dehumanization of the individual in vivid detail. On the positive side, he suggested for society a transformation based on preserving the individual. "Religion [that is, for Kierkegaard Christianity] is the true humanity"; and religious existence—persons personally related to a personal God—rather than to the anonymous "public" is needed if society is to be remade, if the resources for its renewal are to be provided, and if people are to be prevented from being stampeded into impersonal totalitarian movements.

PROBLEM III: STATE, POWER, AND AUTHORITY

Already suggested in the preceding sections is the existentialist's distrust of political power and the state. Too often these become the object of idolatrous adoration and commitment that block individual self-realization. Some of the most forceful statements of this theme are found in the writings of the late nineteenth-century German philosopher, Friedrich Nietzsche (1844–1900), and later existentialists are frequently indebted to Nietzsche in their similar observations.[9]

Nietzsche's thought begins with the observation that "God is dead," and he added that "we have killed him." This widely quoted statement meant for Nietzsche that in the modern scientific and industrial age—the result of men's efforts—the existence of God is no longer believable. To be sure, millions of individuals

[8] Denis de Rougemont, *The Devil's Share*, New York: Pantheon (Bollingen Series), 1944, p. 141.

[9] Most of Nietzsche's writing has some bearing on the topics of this Problem. See especially *Thus Spake Zarathustra* and *Beyond Good and Evil*, both of which are available in many editions and anthologies.

may claim to believe, but the God hypothesis is neither supported by nor relevant to modern culture. Still, the death of God, Nietzsche said, is not an event for rejoicing, for also dead with him are the old theological picture of man and the commitment to values it entailed. In fact, the implication of the death of God for European civilization is a nihilistic loss of all meaning and value.

Nietzsche's problem is to develop a new picture of man without theological assumptions and to restate the conditions for meaningful valuation. His doctrine of man is expressed in the image of the "superman" (*Übermensch*), a morally new type of individual who through dedicated commitments—the "will to power"—will be a creator of values in the very presence of nihilism. The values of the superman will be naturalistic rather than theological, and though Nietzsche spoke of a transvaluation of values, his real concern was to war against accepted valuations that prevent the realization of selfhood and the attainment of culture. Mankind needs courage to live by the highest values, which are the personal or existential qualities of integrity, honesty, and generosity.

Nietzsche was unsure which is the more universal characteristic—fear or laziness. Both keep men from culture and self-realization for men fear social retaliation, and so they do not strive to be uniquely themselves. The State thus appears almost as a Devil in Nietzsche's ethical vision. It intimidates men into conformity and denies them their proper destiny. The State embodies mediocrity rather than fulfillment, and the power it has moves men to conformity. Even more, Nietzsche opposed all overvaluations of political life: it is sheer idolatry to seek salvation in political programs and state power, whether they be democratic, socialist, or communist.

As a philosopher, Nietzsche lacked both systematic commitments and developed premises. His observations on the state and society are largely negative, and one might infer that his position ultimately is political anarchy. Yet Nietzsche's purpose as a writer was—with most existentialists—less to present doctrines than to "disturb" his readers and to issue a call for moral courage and personal integrity. Man's social dimension has an importance appropriate to it, but it is neither the highest dimension nor a self-fulfilling one. In an age tending to absolutize and worship the

State, Nietzsche saw depersonalization and destruction. Only courage and personal valuations can prevent the total loss of the individual.

PROBLEM IV: LAW AND RIGHTS

Insofar as there is a common approach among existentialists to the problem of law and rights, it must be judged to be quite different from those met in other philosophical perspectives. Existentialists have not produced a philosophy of law analogous to those we have studied. Rather, they have dealt with law and rights very indirectly, facing rather the general problem of a "life-order," as Karl Jaspers (1883–1969) called it, whether economic, social, or legal. Jaspers' position, which will be followed, is that the construction and maintenance of any absolutely valid and inclusive life-order is impossible.[10]

Influenced especially by Kierkegaard, Jaspers' voluminous writings seem pledged to the overall goal of breaking down modern man's trust in science, in theology, indeed in rational endeavor anywhere. Offering no philosophic doctrines himself, Jaspers sought to show the limits of science and thereby to loosen man from the fetters of determinate thinking. Yet, it is inaccurate to classify Jaspers as an irrationalist: he suggested that rational thought is really subphilosophical, and that "philosophizing" lies above reason and must replace it.

This polemic against rationalism rests on Jaspers' belief that the foundation of all knowledge is "out of possible Existence"—a truth that rationalism easily forgets. Existence is met in the concrete situation of the striving, existing individual, but such situations are in many ways incompatible with the claims of reason. The world, therefore, is not reducible to a single philosophical principle, and to acknowledge this incompatibility prepares the way for a movement away from the objective world toward Existence.

[10] See *Man in the Modern Age*, tr. Eden and Cedar Paul, London, 1951.

Existence can never be grasped by rationalistic thought: it is the beginning or ground of thought, not an end or object. This means that an existing person cannot be transformed into some kind of impersonal thing. I am "the being who is not, but who can and ought to be and, therefore, decides in time whether he is eternal." That is, one experiences a need to be oneself in an absolute way; one can accept this or sink into nothingness. To exist, therefore, is to be free.

At the highest moments of existence, personality cannot remain satisfied merely with social and legal levels, even though it also cannot forget its roots in the community. This dissatisfaction results in part from the recognition that no steadfast life-order is possible. Life in its expressiveness is always seeking new forms, and even a machinelike organization of society cannot repress it. Furthermore, any given life-order contains internal oppositions, not only of state to state and of class to class, but within life itself, as for example, in the creativity yet destruction of self-interest. Human life, therefore, is impossible in mechanical production and social or legal rational systems. It is possible only as historical destiny, by which Jaspers meant the human effort to bring a world of purposive order into existence. That this is man's task shows that his being is not exhausted in techniques, apparatus, political programs, legal systems, or mass-life.

Problem V: Political Obligation

The problem of political obligation is directed toward the nature and basis of the bond that links individuals and society. That there is such a bond is indisputable, though its moral legitimacy and justification remain as philosophical problems even when the fact is recognized. Men are—and perhaps ought to be—bound and determined by the social order, yet few if any theories omit reference to some limitation on the completeness of such determination. The possibility of rejection, of revolt, is linked with and often is part of the very meaning of man's obligation to society, and may in fact be seen as the more fundamental obligation.

If the fundamental obligations of men are in fact toward freedom and not authority, one may follow Sartre in making violence rather than political submission the fundamental category. For Sartre, scarcity, as we have seen,[11] brings with it a perpetual menace of death, for each individual is a risk of death for the other. When socially organized, this threat takes the form of objective violence by dominant groups of individuals against all other groups. Violence becomes, so to speak, the basic social fact. In the presence of this social fear, Sartre and those influenced by him conclude that the only obligation, indeed necessity, that social existence sanctions is to use violence. It is necessary, that is, that I and my community destroy the menacing *praxis* of the other and his community. This is Sartre's reading of the Marxist doctrine of class struggle.

A somewhat different conclusion from Sartre's, however, is found in the thought of the French writer and Nobel prize winner, Albert Camus (1913–1960).[12] Collaborator with Sartre in the French resistance movement during World War II, Camus broke with his friend over the latter's growing Marxist sympathies and acceptance of violence. To be sure, Camus himself used the possibility of rebellion as the basis for an analysis of man's social and historical existence. Rebellion is a dimension of man's being: it removes the individual from his solitude, thus founding its first value on the whole human race. If a man decides to rebel, it is because he has decided that human society has some value. Rebellion, therefore, Camus observed, is never nihilistic. It is "born of the spectacle of irrationality, confronted with an unjust and incomprehensible condition." The rebel asks not simply for life, but for reasons for living; he thus fights to preserve the integrity of one part of his own being. Rebellion is "the secular will not to surrender"; "it keeps us always erect in the savage, formless movement of history."

And yet, Camus observed, there is a necessary limit to rebellion. Indeed, every thought or action that goes beyond limits

<hr />

[11] See Problem I above.

[12] *The Rebel*, tr. Anthony Bower, New York, 1956.

negates itself. The freedom and justice for which the rebel fights are never simply given. They derive from the conditions of living, which must be accepted along with the suffering entailed by the limits of the possible. The logic of the rebel is to try to serve justice, not to add to injustice, but he must face the tensions resulting from the opposition of violence and nonviolence and of absolute justice and freedom. Violence destroys life and absolute justice destroys freedom. Rebellion without limits means slavery.

The revolutionary mind must therefore return to the only system of thought that is faithful to its origins, namely thought that recognizes limits. Such thought must apply the law of moderation to the contradictions and oppositions of rebellious thought. Moderation teaches that some element of realism is necessary to every ethic, even an ethic of rebellion, and that the irrational poses limits on the rational. Yet moderation must not be viewed as the opposite of rebellion: these are born and can only live in relation to each other, the one finding its limit in the other.

The limit of rebellion, however, is finally met in the "We are" that also must have its place in history. Every form of society presupposes a discipline and an order, but if the "We are" be denied, society and discipline lose all their direction. When rebellion is taken as the sole value, there is no recognition of rights. The absence of rights implies the absence of social obligations, and the absence of obligations denies the possibility of the very values the rebel seeks to realize. Rebellion thus also reveals a limit in human nature itself, namely the limit of man's social dimension and his consequent dependence upon and obligation to the social order. Rebellion, moderation, and society, tragically opposed as they often are, are all conditions for and limitations of each other.

PROBLEM VI: THE IDEAL OF JUSTICE

Various existentialist themes have particular relevance to the problem of justice. Usually viewed as the consummate political and social value, justice is understood in most theories as an order among persons that secures certain conditions for their lives. As an order, it has also frequently been taken as a rational ideal in the sense that rational insight is necessary to and can give the principles of the ideal; as the consummate political value, it has been taken as the "saving" principle for society.

While recognizing the importance of justice to any society, existentialists have certain doubts about it. Their distrust of reason for existential concerns leads them to judge that belief in achieved rationality is illusory. The uncertainties of existence constantly present a challenge to the adequacy of any proposed structure of justice, and the elusiveness of finality means that such structures can never be taken as fully reliable. Man's corruption suggests that rules of justice in any living society can never be wholly free from the self-interests of dominant individuals and groups. In sum, both the nature of existence and the complexity of justice preclude the possibility that full justice is ever achievable, or that confidence in justice will ever be adequate to man's ultimate concerns.

Among the more forceful writers enunciating these themes is the Protestant theologian and social critic, Reinhold Niebuhr (1892–1971).[13] Hardly classifiable as an existentialist—he would reject the appellation in many of its connotations—he nevertheless reflected and developed existentialist themes in his analyses of social issues. Particularly relevant to all discussions of justice for Niebuhr is the complexity of the concept and of its relations to ideals of brotherhood and love.

Justice may be considered in two ways: as a set of abstract rules and as structures of justice within historical conditions. Rules of justice are instruments of community serving to establish obligations that go beyond merely egotistic ones and to develop syntheses of interests. There is no need, Niebuhr believed, to be completely pessimistic about the ability of communities to achieve solutions on these matters. Rules of justice are not merely the product of selfish interests or the unstable compromises of power. The actual structures of justice in society, however, do not fulfill

---

[13] See *The Nature and Destiny of Man*, 2 vols., New York, 1943, *Moral Man and Immoral Society*, New York, 1932, and *Children of Light and Children of Darkness*, New York, 1944.

the law of brotherhood—human sin is the social reality preventing such fulfillment. The harmony achieved by justice can remain only an approximation of brotherhood for three reasons: all rational estimates of rights are infected by the contingent and finite character of human reason; complete impartiality is illusory; and rules of justice—caught in the relativities of history as they are—can never be unconditional.

Yet Niebuhr concluded with a position that is neither relativistic nor pessimistic. There are relativities in the ideals of justice held by various societies, and there are also certain approximately universal rules and duties. There is evidence of progress, but there is also no ground for believing that the transcendent ideal of justice will ever be fully realized—or even known. With the existentialists, Niebuhr affirmed that man is more than a social animal, and that his existence has more than the one social dimension. However important the ideal of justice is, it is not the final source of man's perfection; and the belief that it is, is idolatry.

Bibliographical Essay

A number of fine surveys of existentialist thought have been written; among them are Marjorie Grene, *Dreadful Freedom*, Chicago, 1948; reissued as *Introduction to Existentialism*; Emmanuel Mounier, *Existentialist Philosophies*, New York, 1949; Ronald Grimsley, *Existentialist Thought*, Cardiff, Wales, 1955; Walter A. Kaufmann (ed.), *Existentialism from Dostoevsky to Sartre*, New York, 1956; F. H. Heinemann, *Existentialism and the Modern Predicament*, New York, 1958; H. J. Blackham, *Six Existentialist Thinkers*, New York, 1959; F. Molina, *Existentialism as Philosophy*, Englewood Cliffs, N.J., 1962; and R. G. Olson, *An Introduction to Existentialism*, New York, 1962. These works touch on major figures in the movement as well as on many topics of interest to the social philosopher. Though they are not ordinarily classified as existentialist, the following works may also be mentioned as reflecting certain existentialistic themes: Reinhold Niebuhr, *The Children of Light and the Children of Darkness*, New

York, 1946; John Wild, *Human Freedom and Social Order*, Durham, N.C., 1959; and many books by Paul Tillich.

Still other writers, difficult to classify, have written on social topics and should be mentioned. These include Nicolas Berdyaev, Martin Buber, M. Merleau-Ponty, and Unamuno. Scholars have only recently turned to the social implications of Heidegger's thought, although he is one of the most eminent thinkers in the position. Sartre's later thought is difficult, and two expositions of it may be consulted: Wilfrid Desan, *The Marxism of Jean-Paul Sartre*, Gloucester, Mass., 1974; and Raymond Aron, *History and the Dialectic of Violence*, tr. Barry Cooper, New York, 1975. Articles on existentialist thought as well as phenomenology may be found in the journal *Man and World*.

Linguistic
Philosophy

In many ways an even more radical "revolution" in philosophy than the existentialist protest is the movement variously known as linguistic, ordinary language, and analytic philosophy.[1] The term revolution is used advisedly. Linguistic philosophers claim to present not another doctrine, but a new conception of philosophical activity, which they insist goes to the very nature of philosophy itself.

The most general characterization that can be made of this perspective—and one must be careful of generalizations here for linguistic philosophers, like existentialists, do not form a "school" in the traditional sense—is that philosophy has become language oriented. Linguistic philosophers share the conviction that the perennial problems of philosophy can be clarified, if not resolved, by careful attention to the ways in which languages are actually used. Metaphysical questions, which they believe are never genuine questions at all, are the objects of critical attention. These questions are considered mere confusions resulting when language is used in peculiar and illegitimate ways. Offering no new or "higher" knowledge, philosophy becomes the activity of clarifying and removing the conceptual puzzles into which language can occasionally lead one. No longer is philosophy to be pursued in the "grand manner" of building systems of ultimate propositions: it is rather

[1] In some circles "analytic philosophy" would be the more common term. Preference is given here to "linguistic philosophy" to emphasize the concern with language reflected in this position and, generally, the authority of Ludwig Wittgenstein (on which see further below).

a piecemeal effort to achieve clarity through the resolution of particular issues arising from linguistic confusion.

To say that philosophy is concerned with language is itself no revolutionary statement. Philosophers have always found it important to give careful attention to language and linguistic forms. Linguistic philosophers go further than this: philosophy is the activity of finding meaning, and in no way is it the pursuit of truth. Why should philosophy be so restricted? The first—and earlier—answer was given by a form of linguistic philosophy usually called "logical positivism." Agreeing with the antimetaphysical and scientific stress of earlier positivism,[2] this twentieth-century philosophy began its work with this observation: true and false are terms having application to propositions or statements, but before it is possible to decide whether any given statement is true or false, it is first necessary to know what it means. How can one determine the meaning or sense of a statement? Logical positivists answered: one knows the meaning when one is able to indicate the circumstances under which the statement would be true (or the circumstances that would make it false). The only way the meaning of any sentence can be made clear is to describe these circumstances. Meaning is reference to verification.

Of the many statements that purport to be cognitive, there is a group found in logic and mathematics whose truth can be determined simply by the principle of noncontradiction. Given the meaning of 2, 4, 5, plus, and equals, it is true that $2 + 2 = 4$ and false that $2 + 2 = 5$ because the former is consistent, the latter inconsistent. Unfortunately, however, while these *analytic* propositions are necessarily true or false, they give no knowledge of reality. Their sole function is to relate symbols to each other. The propositions that give knowledge of the world are *synthetic*. Their meaning lies in their relation to possible verification in sense experience. If it is possible to specify the circumstances under which the proposition could be so verified (or falsified), it is meaningful; if it is not possible, the proposition is meaningless and "non-sense." All meaningful synthetic propositions, positivists

[2] The chief influences on logical positivism, however, came mainly from advances in science and logic, not from the positivistic sources used in Chapter Two above. Hume's critique of reason is important for logical positivists also.

assert, belong to the sciences. There are also propositions enunciating value judgments, such as "Lying is wrong." These, however, are neither analytic (since they cannot be proven by their consistency) nor synthetic (since no sense experience could possibly verify them), but *emotive* for they involve the expression of emotion rather than any cognitive function.

With their threefold distinction of types of propositions—analytic, synthetic, and emotive—logical positivists are able to resolve traditional philosophical problems in two ways. Some of them will dissolve away upon analysis: they may look like problems and questions because they are framed in a certain grammatical order, but the words as they are put together do not make logical sense. Secondly, some philosophical problems will prove to be real; but if so, then they are capable of being solved by the methods of science. That is, if such problems are answerable in principle, the answer can be given only by scientific investigation. Thus, the fate of all philosophical problems is that either they will disappear by being shown to be mistakes and misunderstandings in the use of language, or they will be found to be ordinary scientific questions in disguise.

A second and more recent answer to the question of restricting philosophy to language analysis is given by a group of scholars who find traditional philosophy less nonsense than puzzlement. While agreeing with the logical positivists in the rejection of metaphysics and the prevention of linguistic confusion, these philosophers differ from them in three important ways. First, they generally reject the verification principle. For them it is either a kind of metaphysical principle itself or it is extremely narrow in its restriction of cognitive meaning to relation to sense experience. To use a slogan of the position, "the meaning is the use," not the method of verification.[3] Next, linguistic philosophers reject any

---

[3] A more technical way of putting this slogan is this: logical positivists often assumed that meaning must be understood as denotation or naming. Linguistic philosophers recognize, however, that language is exceedingly more complex than this. Attention is therefore given to such problems as how children actually learn to understand an expression. Central to this achievement is the mastery of rules, and hence, the sense or meaning of an expression is the rule for the employment of that expression.

rigid interpretation of the analytic-synthetic distinction. In certain types of discourse, to be sure, this distinction can be maintained, but in actual and living languages, it does not hold. Finally, linguistic philosophers reject any simple classification of uses of language such as cognitive, directive, and emotive, insisting that sentences perform an indefinitely large number of tasks. To use a second slogan, "every statement has its own logic"; that is, the uses and functions of words are richer and more varied than a rigid classification would imply.

The linguistic view of philosophy may now be stated as "conceptual elucidation," which must be pursued to eliminate misconceptions deriving from language itself. Misconceptions arise because, as Professor Gilbert Ryle (1900–1976) has written,[4] some expressions are "systematically misleading." For example, the statement, "Mr. Baldwin is a politician," is not misleading, for it states a fact in a straightforward way. The statement, "Mr. Baldwin is objective," however, though similar in structure, does not exhibit or identify the fact for which it is being used (if any), and is misleading without analysis. The linguistic philosopher holds that traditional philosophy has been particularly susceptible to error because of such expressions, and he seeks to detect "the sources in linguistic idioms of recurrent misconstructions and absurd theories," which he believes is "the sole and whole function of philosophy" (Ryle).

Philosophy thus shifts from questions like, What is the nature of x? to questions like, What does x do in a language, and how does it do it? Elucidation involves the description of the roles of certain concepts and the conditions under which they function. Doubting that philosophers can give any systematic account of reality, analysts may, with G. E. Moore (1873–1958) defend common sense, with Ludwig Wittgenstein (1889–1951) remove philosophical perplexities, with John Wisdom (1904–   ) point out the unique anxieties underlying philosophical puzzles, or with John Austin (1911–1960) search out the ways in which language can be legitimately employed. The general aim is the same, namely

---

[4] See his article, "Systematically Misleading Expressions," *Proceedings of the Aristotelian Society*, 1931–1932.

to clear up puzzlement, to prevent misconceptions in language, and to expose absurd theories.

PROBLEM I: MAN AND SOCIETY

The quest for clarity in social philosophy follows the directions outlined above. Offering no special philosophical wisdom for society, either as a kind of unique knowledge or as higher moral guidance, linguistic philosophers find that many of the central concepts of traditional social philosophy like group, society, state, and law are vague, formless, and misleading. Therefore, their use is accompanied often by perplexity and confusion, which may issue in social theories that are extreme, if not absurd. The logic [5] of these concepts must be properly mapped out if this consequence is to be avoided.

In dealing with concepts like "society" and "community," two initial observations must be made. The first is that societies are not given or recognizable in the way physical objects like stones are— one does not observe them in the same way nor do their corresponding concepts behave logically in the same way. This fact poses interesting questions about the nature of the social sciences as well as about social concepts. As Peter Winch has pointed out, whereas the physical scientist has to deal only with one set of rules, namely those governing his own activity, what the sociologist is studying, as well as his study of it, are both human activities and are therefore carried on according to two sets of rules. Or, as he says elsewhere, "even if it is legitimate to speak of one's understanding of a mode of social activity as consisting in a knowledge of regularities, the nature of this knowledge must be very different from the

[5] This frequently used word suggests an important point that should not be missed. The task of conceptual elucidation must not be confused with the work of the linguist or grammarian. The "logic" of an expression is a matter of the rules governing its coemployment with other expressions in communication situations.

knowledge of physical regularities." [6] Now the difficulties here, as with the concept "society," is that while "society" may be linked with many factual traits like locality, identity of interests, the sense of belonging, and shared values, no such trait seems to be a necessary condition for social existence. In this regard, it is like the concept of "game" which Wittgenstein penetratingly examined: [7] no unique denotation or designation for the concept is to be found.

The second observation to be made is that "society" and "community" seem to express an evaluative as well as an apparent factual meaning—and explanation of the evaluative factor presents further difficulties. An older, German distinction—itself evaluative —separated *Gemeinschaft* and *Gesellschaft*, the first referring to first-person, emotively based communities, the second to functional though often impersonal communities. A survey article of a few decades ago found as many as ninety-four different meanings of community in the field of sociology alone.[8] Part of the meaning of this concept, it appears, is parasitic on our general social and moral attitudes.

But how, then, shall "society" best be understood? Again following the lead of Wittgenstein, many linguistic and analytic philosophers have answered that societies are numbers of individuals held together in an order maintained through rules or norms. Such rules are expressive of human desires and perform two basic functions: they define the rights and duties individuals have toward each other, and—since the concept of human action involves "following a rule"—they make possible the domain of human acts. "Society" and "community" are thus seen to be relation structures under rules. Given this move, linguistic philosophers have gone on to provide elucidations of related concepts like group, status, institution, authority, and power. The result of their

[6] *The Idea of a Social Science*, London, 1958, pp. 87–88. Winch's work has generated an extensive literature on the methodology of social science which the student will find valuable to consult. The observations in the text may also profitably be compared with the view on science in Chapter 2.

[7] In the first pages of his *Philosophical Investigations*. The importance of these pages for contemporary philosophy can hardly be overexaggerated.

[8] Richard Hillery, "Definitions of Community," *Rural Sociology*, 1955.

work is not so much to offer new facts about man and society as a social scientist might do, but to provide the clarifications of meaning that can serve as a prolegomenon to further exploration of factual relationships.

PROBLEM II: SOCIAL AND POLITICAL VALUES

For linguistic philosophers, philosophic discussion about values is discussion of the language of values. Offering neither prescriptions for individuals or society nor possessing any higher wisdom concerning ethical and political values, they rather attempt to clarify the logic of statements expressing valuations. That these statements require special clarification seems obvious enough. To say that one ought not to steal or that laws should be just, is to make neither a logical nor an empirical assertion: not logical, for its truth cannot be determined by logical analysis alone; not empirical, for no fact seems to be asserted and no factual verification can be given.

The first attempts by linguistic philosophers to analyze value sentences followed the logical positivist's classificaton of cognitive, emotive, and imperative uses of language. Since they are obviously not cognitive nor do they take the form of commands, value sentences fall under the heading of emotive, and the resultant theory is called emotivism. According to this theory, a judgment like "stealing is wrong" really makes no assertion at all: it is an expression of the speaker's emotion. Roughly translated, it would mean, "I dislike stealing," and its role in language would be similar to an interjection.

Later linguistic philosophers, however, find this emotivism an oversimplification. It gives no explanation of the fact that people disagree and dispute over ethical judgments, and it overlooks the influence that such judgments have on the conduct of people. More subtle analysis is therefore needed, and many linguistic philosophers have fulfilled this need. One influential theory has

been developed by J. O. Urmson in his article, "On Grading." [9]
To call things good or bad, Urmson wrote, is to grade them, as for
example apples might be graded in terms of their qualities. Such
grading is not simply an interjection, it is an act—the making of a
choice—with a commitment to similar choices in like situations.
A second theory is that of R. M. Hare (1919–   ),[10] who distinguished descriptive and prescriptive uses of language. Ethical
statements are clearly not descriptive but prescriptive, and hence
they function as imperatives or commendations.

A third set of observations has been made about values by
Professor W. B. Gallie (1912–   ) which includes a further issue
beyond linguistic analysis.[11] Values, he wrote, have varied greatly
in different societies; how can one interpret these differences? Or,
more simply, is morality one or many? Analyzing the question, he
found that four answers have been given to it. The "monarchic"
view says that only one set of moral canons exists, that only one
right judgment about values is possible. Yet there are many possibilities for error in judgment, which explain the differences in
men's moral and political beliefs. The "polyarchic" view suggests
that there is not one but an indefinite number of value standards,
and that therefore there are many fundamentally different moralities. Ethical relativism is like the polyarchic view in admitting a
number of moral standards, but differs in holding that they are
always relative to other and more basic differences (for example,
economic differences) among groups of people. Finally, idealism
teaches that there is one absolute, eternal morality that inevitably
differentiates itself into distinct forms or phases. The issue of one
or many moralities is the most important question facing moral
philosophy, Professor Gallie argued. He suggested, however, that
logical analysis alone does not settle it, for it is also a question
of fact. His own hypothesis was that certain facts do attest to the
polyarchic view, which implies that it is possible to say that both
sides in a value dispute are right in at least some of their claims.

[9] *Mind*, 59 (1950), pp. 145–69.

[10] *The Language of Morals*, Oxford, 1952.

[11] "Liberal Morality and Socialist Morality," *Philosophy*, 24 (1949).

The actual political and social values which have received the attention of linguistic philosophers include such traditional ones as liberty, equality, justice, and welfare. Particular analyses of these ideals differ from philosopher to philosopher, yet some generalization about them is possible. Political ideals belong basically to the class of prescriptive, not descriptive concepts, for they involve commendations and presumptions. Equality, for example, does not describe the human condition but rather commends a certain attitude toward it. These ideals also have a variety of meanings and uses, and part of the philosophical task is to explore such uses in their different contexts. They also have relations to other social concepts like rights, power, and authority which need clarification. And finally, there is the philosophical task of evaluating the justificatory arguments offered in support of them.

Problem III: State, Power, and Authority

From the time of Bodin, at least, much of social philosophy has centered on issues concerning the state, power, and authority or—as Bodin put it—on sovereignty. Yet many contemporary political theorists have abandoned the concept, seeking to develop their views without it. One philosophical observer, Professor W. J. Rees (1914–   ), believes there has been a twofold reason for this: sovereignty is subject to conceptual confusions and logical difficulties; and, partly related thereto, it is a difficult concept to apply to the complex political organizations of the modern world. The task of the philosopher, therefore, is to clarify the concept and the questions pertaining to it.[12]

Consider the question, Is it necessary that there should be a sovereign in every state? A linguistic philosopher like Professor Rees invites his readers to consider the kind of question this is.

[12] See his article, "The Theory of Sovereignty Restated," *Mind*, 59 (1950).

Is it a genuine question, that is, one that does not rule out a possible answer because of logical contradictions (What is there outside the universe?), or one that does not indicate what kind of information is relevant to an answer (Is everything twice as big today as it was yesterday?)? Questions about sovereignty do not seem to involve these difficulties, but they are affected by another complication: they are really complex questions, actually involving many rather than one question. Therefore, Professor Rees argues, it is necessary to clarify the key terms in questions about sovereignty, and then to replace the complex questions with unambiguous ones to which answers can be given.

Six different uses of the term sovereign are specified in Rees' article. Sovereign may refer to (1) the supreme legal authority, (2) the supreme legal authority in so far as it is also a moral authority, (3) a coercive power exercised by a determinate body, (4) a coercive power exercised by all the members of a community, (5) the strongest political influence in a community, and (6) the permanent interest therein. Since the concept state is closely related to sovereignty and is often used with it, Rees also distinguishes three of its meanings as (1) a politically organized society, (2) a politically organized society in so far as it is ideally organized, and (3) government considered as an institution. In terms of these distinctions, it is possible to give real answers to the traditional questions about sovereignty and therewith also to retain the concept for possible use in current political theory.

The concepts of power and authority, which are closely related to sovereignty, have also been carefully examined for their meaning and conceptual relationships. To be sure, they are central concepts in many sociological investigations as well, though the philosopher's concern with them is primarily elucitory. The search for the concept of power is one to aid an understanding of the relation between A and B when it is said, A has power over B, particularly as power over B means or entails action against B's real interests.[13] The concept of authority, on the other hand, must be distinguished from power, for power seems to be what is resorted to when authority breaks down. Indeed, as Peter Winch has sug-

[13] So put in Steven Lukes' *Power, A Radical View*, London, 1974—though other philosophers have found this meaning too limited.

gested in his influential study of the concept,[14] authority is related to human interests, and he has tried to show this by relating authority to an understanding of society as rule governed organization. The acceptance of authority (and one seldom "accepts" power) is not something which, as a matter of fact, can be dispensed with, for to participate in rule governed activities is in a certain way to accept authority. And why? Because such participation means accepting that there is a right and a wrong way of doing things that does not depend on one's own caprice.[15]

PROBLEM IV: LAW AND RIGHTS

One of the most frequently asked questions takes the form, What is *x*? In many circumstances, this form causes no special difficulty, yet it can occasion a whole series of perplexities and confusions. This happens when one believes that his answer to it is a real or "true" definition giving the "essential nature" of the term being defined. An example would be, What is law?, with the answer, It is the command of a sovereign—an answer purporting to be the true definition of law.

Yet, this effort to find a true definition is misplaced for, linguistic philosophers believe, it is connected with failures to understand meaning and symbolism. It is, in fact, an effort resulting from a number of errors about language. First among them is the belief that there is some kind of *real connection* between a word and an object, so that words are taken to have "proper" meanings. A second error results from thinking that the use of a word *guarantees* that the fact or object to which it refers exists. A third arises from a conviction or assumption that words have a *magical use* to affect the course of natural events. And a fourth error of

[14] "Authority," *Proceedings of the Aristotelian Society*, Supp. Vol. 32 (1958).

[15] As has been frequently noted, linguistic philosophers do not have a common platform. For a position contrary to Winch's, see Robert Paul Wolff's *In Defense of Anarchism*, New York, 1970, which argues that individuality and autonomy are inconsistent with all concepts of authority.

symbolism occurs when one uses a word with *no referent* in mind at all. All of these errors follow from the root mistake of the "proper meaning fallacy," or overlooking the fact that the meaning of words is *conventional*, not real, causal, or natural.

Another group of mistakes follows upon these errors of symbolism. They concern confusions among types of questions, especially verbal, factual, and value ones. An important need for conceptual clarity is to distinguish these types of questions, for language often conceals them. Thus, for example, one asks about the nature of *x*—but is this factual? Usually it is not. It is a request for a definition of a word. One may also search for definitions on the supposition that there is a natural basis of classification, hoping thereby that one's definition reflects the objective structures of things. Or, putting the same point somewhat more technically, one may in his definitions seek the "natural essences" of things. But this is false procedure: neither natural essences nor natural classifications exist—they are the result of language functions.

In discussions of law and rights, theorists are especially prone to error because they seem to gravitate toward questions like, What is law? and What is a right? Answers to these and related questions involve theories of meaning—although it does not follow that they are reducible in toto to linguistic questions. They are therefore questions of considerable importance to philosophers, and they call out for analytic clarification.

Initially, law is definable as the rule system of an actual society. But as such, law seems to exist in at least three different senses, each of which is problematic.[16] There is law as a type of social institution, there are rules of law as distinct from types or standards, and there is *the law* as a source of certain rights and duties granted to individuals. The meaning and status of each of these senses need careful elaboration. Then there is the question of the relation of law to a given society. The command theory, for example, assumed that law exists wherever a people has developed habits of obedience to a sovereign. Critics of this view, however, have suggested that law does not exist unless the population accepts a rule giving authority to those who exercise power. Another issue

[16] This discussion follows R. M. Dworkin's introduction to *The Philosophy of Law*, Oxford, 1977.

prominent in recent literature is the question whether, in order for a system of rules to count as law, the system must obey certain procedural guidelines, or whether the rules enforced by a government must themselves have a moral content. The first of these criteria is sometimes related to the question of the "validity" of law (the basis upon which a law is binding), the second relates to the "value" of law or the "good" law is to serve.

The question of rights raises similar issues. Like law, rights are related to social rules which prescribe behavior, and their basis is found in their correlation with duties. The right of X is the duty of Y,[17] a statement which prescribes behavior and which is normative as well. So understood, the concept of rights possesses meaning in the context of rules and not, as legal positivists try to assert, in the context of factual descriptions. But human experiences, and therewith social rules, are subject to growth and development, and it therefore follows that no single formula, however complex, can determine all the conditions in which the right will hold or, as well, all the conditions that would defeat it. After philosophic clarification must come the appeal to social and legal experience in which some of these conditions, at least, can be determined.

Linguistic philosophers have given great attention to problems of law, and though much of their work aligns them with the school of analytic jurisprudence, they have had a general influence on philosophy of law. Some observers, in fact, have suggested that linguistic philosophy is most at home in this area of social philosophy. In any case, its contributions here are significant.

PROBLEM V: POLITICAL OBLIGATION

That linguistic philosophers find much of traditional political theory to consist of verbal definitions and strange uses of ordinary

---

[17] An earlier, preanalytic philosophy clarification of the relationships of right, duty, and similar concepts was provided by W. N. Hohfeld. His work, *Fundamental Legal Conceptions*, New Haven, 1919, is often still the starting point in legal discussions.

words is now apparent. Still, if this be the understanding of philosophic statements about society, one can ask what kind of propositions they really are, and why—if they do not express fact—people use them. There is, in other words, a need to understand the effects of certain kinds of political language even when they give no scientific information. In an earlier but still influential paper, Margaret Macdonald (1905?–1956) utilized the Wittgensteinian view that philosophical statements function as linguistic recommendations to deal with the question of political obligation.[18] Predicting nothing about behavior and empty of fact, philosophical statements about obligation, she found, are invitations to "picture" facts in various (and sometimes strange) ways.

Miss Macdonald believed that different pictures of political relations, such as those offered by contract and organic theories, carry with them their own psychological effects and suggest, therefore, alternative insights into situations. In this regard, philosophical remarks are more like poetry than, say, scientific analogy; people are led to use them because of their psychological effects even though nothing can be learned about political affairs from them. This likeness to poetry (but philosophy *is not* poetry) helps to explain the peculiarity and puzzlement of political theory.

The authors of traditional political theories see themselves doing more than writing poetry; they are seeking explanations to the problems of social life. Perhaps the most basic of social problems concerns political obligation, and to it have been given a number of proposed solutions. Consent theorists point to an original binding contract; idealists posit a higher self from which issue obligations of self-realization in society; and utilitarians suggest the advantage of society as the ground of obligation. Upon examination, Miss Macdonald found each of these theories to be wanting. Contract theory leads to no empirical original; the higher self is misleading in talking of a person one can never meet; and utilitarianism reduces to the tautology that only the governments we ought to support are those we ought to support because they promote the social good.

[18] See her "The Language of Political Theory," *Proceedings of the Aristotelian Society*, 41, 1940–1941. This view of philosophy was also influenced by the contemporary British philosopher, John Wisdom.

What is the secret of this ineptitude? Two observations help to answer this question. The first is that the use to which traditional theorists put language is confusing and illegitimate. The second is that theorists are searching for *general* answers to the questions they put. Such general answers are really metaphysical for they are offered as unique and almost magical formulas to resolve inquiry. Such formulas are impossible and unnecessary: there are only specific solutions to specific questions.

These observations apply to the problem of political obligation. To the question, Why ought I obey?, no general answer can be given. Obedience is related to particular matters such as a given law or a special authority, and only varied and shifting criteria are available for these situations. At this point, in fact, many traditional theories supply valuable insights since there are situations where consent, ideals, or consequences do offer the criteria for answering questions about obedience. But to ask about obedience in general is to ask a senseless question, and of course the answer to a senseless question is itself without sense. Responsible citizens, Miss Macdonald concluded, can never know once and for all what their political duties are, "and so we can never go to sleep."

Problem VI: The Ideal of Justice

Like so many basic social and political concepts, justice stands in need of analytic clarification and elucidation. Perhaps the most important recent account of this ideal is found in the writings of Professor H. L. A. Hart (1907–   ). Proper attention to the concept, he has said, shows that while it is a concept of appraisal, it belongs to a distinct section of moral words. Justice seems to have a special character and to be more specific than such more general words as good and bad. Its closest relative seems to be "fair" and—for injustice—"unfair." This is easily shown by the fact that while many words of commendation cannot be substituted for just, fair usually can.

Yet analysis has not gone far enough merely in noting this

relation to fairness. It is necessary, Hart argued, to find the specific character of justice. This is done by observing that the principle justice denotes is that individuals are entitled to a certain relative position of equality or inequality in respect to each other (hence the traditional interpretation of justice as balance or proportion). In simpler words, the central idea in the concept of justice is to "treat like cases alike and different cases differently." Even this statement needs to be supplemented, however, for appraisals of law as just or unjust require knowledge of what similarities and differences among human beings are relevant.

Hence it is necessary to distinguish two parts of the idea of justice. The first part is the invariant formal principle expressed by treating like cases alike. Sound as this principle is, it is by itself useless for criticizing law apart from the second element in justice, namely a criterion by which to determine when cases are alike or different. The first part of justice is close in meaning to the idea of proceeding by a rule without bias and is relatively stable. The criterion of relevant differences, however, is a varying criterion and depends on nonlegal factors as well. The reason for this is that the law itself cannot say what similarities and differences the law must recognize. Differences in political and moral outlooks are reflected in the formulation and application of this criterion.

Justice, Professor Hart concluded, is thus a specific form of excellence attributed to laws. His analysis shows that it is a value distinct from other values and may, in fact, conflict with some of them such as the general welfare. Nevertheless, the analytic techniques he applied to the ideal of justice seek to bring greater clarity to the understanding of the ideal itself, as well as to certain puzzles that may arise as men apply the ideal in the concrete appraisals of laws and decisions.

In addition to such a general account of justice, linguistic philosophers have sought to clarify the relation of justice, not only to law and government (which may seem to be its primary home), but also to the social and economic order. When considered in this context, the ideal may be called social justice. Since, as was made clear above, justice is generally related to such other concepts as equality and fairness, the philosophical problem of social justice is primarily one of working out the logic of these three concepts as applicable to the social order. Interesting debates have developed among linguistic philosophers on the bearing of social justice to merit or desert and to human needs, as well as in the economic order to earnings and taxation ("economic justice"). While a "platform" among linguistic philosophers on these and other social questions is not forthcoming, their desire to understand meaning and to seek clarification without confusion unites them in a common philosophical effort.

Bibliographical Essay

Introductory textbooks reflecting logical positivism include Arthur Pap, *Elements of Analytic Philosophy*, New York, 1949; Hans Reichenbach, *The Rise of Scientific Philosophy*, Berkeley, 1951; and Richard von Mises, *Positivism: A Study in Human Understanding*, Cambridge, Mass., 1951. The classic work of the movement is A. J. Ayer's *Language, Truth and Logic*, 2d ed., London, 1949. Many important papers are collected in such anthologies and compilations as H. Feigl and W. Sellars (eds.), *Readings in Philosophical Analysis*, New York, 1949; H. Feigl and M. Brodbeck (eds.), *Readings in the Philosophy of Science*, New York, 1953; *International Encyclopedia of Unified Science*; and the *Minnesota Studies in the Philosophy of Science*. A. J. Ayer's *Logical Positivism*, Glencoe, Ill., 1959, is a broad anthology with excellent bibliographical material.

Analytic philosophy of the more recent linguistic variety is treated in such works as A. J. Ayer and others, *The Revolution in Philosophy*, London, 1956; J. O. Urmson, *Philosophical Analysis*, Oxford, 1956; J. Passmore, *A Hundred Years of Philosophy*, London, 1957; D. F. Pears (ed.), *The Nature of Metaphysics*, London, 1957; and G. J. Warnock, *English Philosophy Since 1900*, London, 1958. Somewhat more advanced is F. Waismann, *The Principles of Linguistic Philosophy*, London, 1965. Anthologies of important discussions from an analytic point of view are: A. G. N. Flew (ed.), *Logic and Language*, Oxford, 1951, and later; M. Macdonald (ed.), *Philosophy and Analysis*, Oxford, 1954; C. A. Mace (ed.), *British*

Philosophy in the Mid-Century, London, 1957; and Morris Weitz (ed.), *20th-Century Philosophy: The Analytic Tradition*, New York, 1966.

The important studies in social philosophy of linguistic philosophers have been collected in the series, P. Laslett (ed.), *Philosophy, Politics and Society*, Oxford, 1956, P. Laslett and W. G. Runciman (eds.), *Philosophy, Politics and Society*, Second Series, Oxford, 1962, and others. An early comprehensive treatment of social philosophy under the influence of Wittgenstein was T. D. Weldon's *The Vocabulary of Politics*, Hardmondsworth, England, 1953; but in many ways the standard text in the field is S. I. Benn and R. S. Peters, *The Principles of Political Thought*, New York, 1959, 1965. While this volume contains no bibliography, the notes may be consulted for a survey of works by linguistic philosophers. Also influential is Brian Barry's *Political Argument*, New York, 1965. Philosophy of law has received special attention in this school. Two valuable works, not limited in scope to linguistic philosophy however, are Richard E. Flathman, *The Practice of Rights*, Cambridge, 1976, and Ronald Dworkin, *Taking Rights Seriously*, Cambridge, Mass., 1977. *Wittgenstein and Justice*, Berkeley, 1972, by Hanna F. Pitkin, contains a survey of Wittgenstein's position and develops some of its implications for social philosophy. Richard T. De George has prepared an important bibliography on authority and related topics in R. Baine Harris (ed.), *Authority: A Philosophical Analysis*, University of Alabama, 1976. Especially important journals for this movement are *Mind*, *Nous*, and *Philosophy and Public Affairs*. The journal *Philosophy of the Social Sciences* is not limited to linguistic and analytic philosophy but many of its articles show an analytic influence.

Platonism

In the presentation of Classical Realism, frequent reference was made to the philosophy of Plato. Although much of Plato's influence on Western social philosophy has been felt through this tradition, it should not be inferred that Platonism is only an antecedent to realism. While this influence is strong—and Aristotle was a student at Plato's Academy for twenty years—Platonism is in fact a distinct position which has had an independent importance through centuries of philosophic activity. In fact, the twentieth century philosopher, A. N. Whitehead, was led by this importance to write that "the safest characterization of the European philosophical tradition is that it consists of a series of footnotes to Plato." [1]

But these footnotes, if some few exceptions to the generalization are allowed, have not led to an expression of Platonism in explicit social theories: no Platonic philosophy of law, for example, has really been developed, nor has much of Platonism been related to or adopted in actual social practice. The Plato scholar, A. E. Taylor, points out such a relation only in the indirect influence of Plato's *Laws* on early Roman law.[2] Rather, it seems, the domination of Plato over Western philosophic thought is to be found in his influence on other philosophers who, like Aristotle, wrestled with Plato's theories and conclusions as they were formulating their own positions. While almost every philosophical tradition has

[1] *Process and Reality*, New York, 1929, p. 63.
[2] *Plato: The Man and his Work*, 6th ed., New York, 1952, p. 495.

been in the same position as Aristotle, idealism should be mentioned as another perspective especially indebted to Plato.

Though much in his writings relates to social issues, three works, *The Republic*, *Statesman*, and *Laws*, are primarily devoted to social philosophy. *The Republic*, perhaps Plato's most widely read book, addresses the problem of justice, though in discussing it, Plato was led to give a comprehensive statement of his philosophy as he had developed it in his middle years. The *Statesman* is a later dialogue on the meaning of statesmanship; and the *Laws*, a work of Plato's old age, is again a broad presentation of his philosophy with particular emphasis on the nature of law and its proper role in society.

Basic to understanding these works—indeed, basic to Platonism itself—is not a social theory, however, but rather a metaphysical vision within which the most distinctive doctrine is the theory of forms. It will be recalled that this concept was central for Aristotle too: form is the principle of kind or structure, determining *what* any individual thing is. Plato had earlier [3] come to this understanding of form, though unlike Aristotle, who made the formal principle part of the natures of things, Plato argued that forms are distinct from the concrete things they qualify. Forms constitute a separate dimension or world that is more real than the world of things, that is the real object of knowledge, and that defines the good of individual things. [4]

What is the theory of forms? Consider Plato's argument as he developed it in *The Republic*. In pursuing the general problem of the dialogue, the nature of justice, Plato was led to assert that justice will be achieved only when mankind has knowledge of justice. But what is knowledge? In seeking at least a partial answer to this question, Socrates, spokesman in the dialogue, points out that there is a difference, for example, between a dreamer and

[3] And perhaps from the Pythagoreans who preceded him.

[4] Plato presented and discussed this theory many times in his writings, and he even examined major objections that can be raised against it. The problem of the separate status of the forms is among these issues, and extensive scholarly debate over Plato's mature position on the status of the forms has continued for centuries. Most standard commentaries on Plato discuss this issue.

a knower. Dreamers mistake appearances for reality, whereas those who know have the real as the object of their thought. But again, it can be asked what this real is. Now, Socrates asserts, the real must be something which *is*: it cannot not-be. Consider as an illustration any natural thing, a stone, a frog, even a human being: in describing such a thing, one must say of it that it was not, it is, it will not be—and the "not's" refer to nonbeing. None of these things, in fact nothing that is found in nature, qualifies as really real, for nonbeing enters into their descriptions, and being or the real always is.

But Socrates would have us make another observation. In addition to these individual things, there are classes or kinds of things—stones, frogs, human beings. Each of these words refers to a group of beings, constituted as a group by the common possession of a structure or form which makes each group to be what it is and not something else. In the illustration above these structures may be called stoneness, frogness, and human nature. Now what happens to them as particular stones or frogs come and go? Plato's answer is, nothing. True enough, the forms must be known by the "mind's eye," for they cannot be sensed; but they are for Plato permanent and immutable, and hence they fulfill the meaning of what it is to be real. Thus in his metaphysics Plato was led to a dualistic vision of the natural and changing world and the real world of forms. Every kind of natural being has its appropriate formal principle in which it "participates" and which gives it the degree of reality it has.

Plato carried this dualism of particular and form over into the realm of values as well. The particular acts of courage or justice, for example, which individuals and states may perform are acts of courage or justice by virtue of their appropriate forms. Similarly, beautiful things are beautiful by virtue of their participation in the real and objective form of beauty. There are forms of value, and in fact every form, even of natural things, fulfills a normative function in Plato's philosophy. A frog is a good frog insofar as and to the degree that it fully embodies the form of frogness; and a state is just to the degree that it embodies the form of justice. And, finally, the theory of forms served an epistemological function for Plato, for forms answer the question of the object of knowledge. One knows frogs, or human beings, or societies, when one has an intellectual grasp of the appropriate form for each kind of thing.

It is within the context of this metaphysical theory that Plato sought to understand the nature of society and the meaning of human life. Accepting, as did Aristotle, the Greek assumption that man is a social animal, Plato argued that the good society is a kind of moral organism which reflects the structure and needs of human nature, educates men toward their proper fulfillment, and orders their interactions under justice. In *The Republic*, in fact, the parallel between the *psyche* or soul and society is made quite explicit, for society is the soul "writ large." The three parts [5] of the soul are the appetites, the "spirited element," and reason; the essential parts of society are economic activity, security or protection, and rulership. Such "parts" reflect the essential structures, the forms, of man and society.

Now the good for both man and society, as for all things, is to function and act according to their essential natures or forms. And as Plato understood these forms, he concluded that reason in man and knowledge for society are their highest acts or functions. To be sure, there are goods appropriate to the other parts: temperance for desire and economic activities, courage for the spirited element and society's protective forces of police and soldiers. But knowledge and wisdom are the highest goods for man; and Plato argued that the good man and the good society both achieve their excellence by ordering themselves under the guidance and rule of reason.

But Plato also recognized that the achievement of good is difficult, and that some human beings may not be sufficiently equipped by nature to possess wisdom.[6] Society must therefore not

---

[5] Or perhaps better, springs of action. Scholars have pointed out that Plato's doctrine here is not to be read as a scientific psychology, nor is it even original in Plato. In distinguishing parts in the soul and in society, Plato was taking note of rival sources of action in human conduct.

[6] In some meanings of the word, Plato was elitist: he did not believe that all men have equal capacities for reason. Partly on this ground, Plato also suggested the practice of eugenics which might lead to the birth of "better" human beings.

only supply the essential services necessary to human life, but it must also order human beings on the basis of their natures (some for economic activity, some for the soldierly life, and some for rulership) and be an educative agent in the achievement of individual virtue. When the parts or classes in society function coherently and in unity under reason, the social good can be realized.[7]

Such functioning will be possible, however, only when political power is united with wisdom. Plato believed in the inherent authority of reason, and he expressed this belief in his theory of the philosopher-king. This concept captures most of Plato's social vision, for it expresses his conviction that the ideal form of statesmanship is rule by the man who has true knowledge of the "tendance of the soul" and of the goods appropriate to human life. Such leadership, should it ever be realized, would be an "aristocracy" in the etymological sense of rule by the best. Other types of social order where this ideal is not present were of course recognized by Plato. Timocracy is rule by the military with honor and courage the highest social virtues. An oligarchy is a society in which wealth rules and where the highest values are those connected with economic activities. The most extreme perversions of aristocracy, however, are democracy and tyranny. Democracy, which for Plato meant "mob-rule," refers to a society where everyone wants to rule and no one wants to be ruled, that is, where no principle of authority is recognized at all. And tyranny, the worst possible form of rule, is a state in which some irrational passion has seized both ruler and citizens and which drives society toward irrational deeds.

In addition to viewing knowledge and education as central to society, Plato recognized the critical role of good laws and legislation. However much philosopher-kings have achieved true knowledge, law and legislation are still indispensable, for rulers cannot provide individual direction in all cases. Especially in the *Laws*, Plato gave detailed attention to the development of laws which would reflect reason and virtue, order society to the common good

---

[7] Plato gave much attention to educational matters in both *The Republic* and the *Laws*, for he took education (along with good laws) to be a primary means toward the attainment of social good.

and individuals to civic virtue, and censor elements disruptive of order and virtue.[8]

Little can be found in Plato that approximates a theory of individual rights or a modern theory of the nature and limits of political obligation. One dialogue, the *Crito*, discusses obligation rather dramatically in the context of Socrate's trial and execution, but concludes with the assertion of a binding obligation to society. The setting of the *Crito* is Socrate's prison: he had been sentenced to death on charges of teaching false doctrine and corrupting the youth. Friends of Socrates, however, had arranged for his escape and urged him to do so, even arguing that "you are not at all justified, Socrates, in betraying your own life when you might be saved." But the laws "speak" to Socrates, urging him not to accept this offer:

> *"Tell us, Socrates," they say; "what are you about? are you not going by an act of yours to overturn us—the laws, and the whole state, as far as in you lies? Do you imagine that a state can subsist and not be overthrown, in which the decisions of law have no power, but are set aside and trampled upon by individuals?"*

Socrates was unwilling to take an easy escape, even on the pretext of a bad law producing a bad judgment against him. The bonds of social obligation are more basic than the mere right or wrong of legal judgment, and Socrates will not escape "to return evil for evil, and injury for injury."

But perhaps the ultimate ground for this refusal to escape is the Socratic-Platonic conception of the consummate social (and individual) virtue, namely, justice. The basic object of Plato's search in *The Republic*, justice must be added to the list of social virtues given above, temperance, courage, and wisdom, to complete the picture of the inclusive social good. For Plato, justice means differentiation of functions and their perfect discharge under the statesmen who guide the state. It involves "minding one's own

---

[8] The vexing problem of censorship, particularly of art and religion, arises at this point in Plato's theories of society and education. Nearly all studies of his thought examine this problem; see the Bibliographical Essay.

business" in the twofold sense of the term: doing the business, discharging the functions, for which nature and education have equipped one; and not trying to do the business for which one is not equipped. The result of this kind of functioning or activity is the realization of an ideal of a coherent and self-controlled life, for individuals as well as for society. While Plato's conception of justice is not, then, the classic formulas of "to each his due" and "treating equals as equal," he provided a philosophical background from which they could emerge.

Bibliographical Essay

Some materials on Plato are mentioned in the Bibliographical Essay on Classical Realism, including books by Barker, Brumbaugh, Grube, and Taylor. Specialized studies on all aspects of Plato's thought, from ethics and education to religion, have been produced, although it should be emphasized that little can be more rewarding than the reading of Plato's own works. The dialogues mentioned in this Appendix, *The Republic*, the *Statesman*, and the *Laws*, are the major texts of Platonic social philosophy. Students seeking more advanced and recent studies of Plato, with reference to contemporary philosophical movements, should consult such studies as those by J. N. Findlay, Eric A. Havelock, and Gilbert Ryle. The most detailed recent treatment of Plato social and legal philosophy is undoubtedly Glenn R. Morrow's *Plato's Creton City, A Historical Interpretation of the Laws*, Princeton, 1960.

Plato's social theories have been given not only extensive commentary, but in the twentieth century they have as well been subject to sometimes vicious attacks. These attacks have centered largely on the question of whether Plato was a totalitarian, and they have referred to such Platonic emphases as the unity of the state, the denial of individual rights, the regimentation of social classes, a suggestion of inquisition in the *Laws*, and the acceptance of censorship. Among the critics have been J. J. Chapman, Warner

Fite, R. H. S. Crossman, and K. R. Popper. The best survey of all these critiques, together with judicial appraisals of them, is still the study by Ronald B. Levinson, *In Defense of Plato*, Cambridge, Mass., 1953.

Fascism

While fascism has been a major political doctrine in the twentieth century, its character and qualifications as a philosophical position are extremely doubtful. Most historians agree that fascism is primarily an eclectic theory which borrows extensively (and often with little understanding) from a number of philosophic sources and then attempts to blend these elements together, seldom with great coherence. Rather than being a philosophy, fascism seems rather a commingling of philosophic ideas serving as a political platform. The influence of irrationalism, more in German than in Italian theories perhaps, also make it difficult to classify fascism as a philosophy. Still, there are philosophical elements in fascism which merit its inclusion in this *Handbook*, if only as an appendix.

The word fascism is derived from *fasciare*, which means to bind or to develop. Originally an Italian movement—and German fascists added little to the theory [1]—the word was used for a doctrine that would wield the Italian people into an organic entity under an all powerful leader and maintain and expand the traditions of ancient Rome. To this end the fascists posited what is undoubtedly their most fundamental thesis, namely, that a people or society is an organic unity, a totality, with a life and destiny

---

[1] The chief modifications of fascism in Germany were five: a greater stress on irrationalism, emphasis on the *Volk* or people as basic, the myth of the Aryan race, strengthening of leadership in the *Führer* principle, and the systematic use of terror.

of its own. Society, they argued, is not merely a sum of individuals, nor is it merely a means for individual self-fulfillment. These liberal doctrines defined the *Ich-Zeit*, the I-time, of the nineteenth century; the twentieth century is to be the *Wir-Zeit*, the time of the we. Thus, individuals exist for society, not for themselves—they are the means relative to ends which are social.

The grounds offered for this conception are many. That society is more than a collection of individuals is shown by history: societies endure through generations, while any individual is but one member of one generation. Language, tradition, and culture give an identity to society to which individuals, to be sure, may make their contributions, but which basically determines the nature and quality of an individual life. Furthermore, men have spiritual finalities—and fascists oppose the materialism of Marxism as strongly as the atomism of liberalism—which can be achieved solely in, and through the resources of, society. Only by sacrificing what is private and by acknowledging the substantiality and reality of the social organism can men reach the self-realization appropriate to themselves as social and spiritual beings.

Thus opposed to all individualistic conceptions, fascism posits a set of social and individual values derived from its organicism. All values have their basis in the social whole—none exists outside it; and liberal conceptions of value are rejected. Egalitarianism for the fascist is simply a lie, for leaders and great men are produced by great societies; and liberty is not ascribable to individuals since its meaning is found in the full expression of a nation's life. Rather, the values for individual and society are those of membership and action: duty, which Mussolini often called the highest of all values, then obedience, responsibility, heroism, and holiness. Indeed, it is because of the stress on these organicist values that fascists speak of their doctrine as first and foremost an ethical one.

But it is in the theory of state, power, and authority that fascism has made its most fateful contributions. Again opposing both political liberalism with its view that the state is an agent of a people's happiness and the Marxist view that the state is an instrument of class oppression which must be abolished, fascism insists that the state *is* a society or people organized and expressing itself. In fact, it is the state which is primary, not society,[2] and the latter depends on the state for its fulfillment, even for its very being. The state, then, is not to be construed in any negative way, but must rather be taken as a spiritual force, active for a people, and constituting the true reality of the individual.

To this political organicism fascist theory adds elements from the absolutist tradition, particularly in its leadership principle. The will, even consciousness, of a people or state finds expression in the will and power of one leader (*Il Duce, Der Führer*) who is capable of rising above private interests and who is the personal embodiment of the spirit of his people. He is the source of all law, though himself not subject to law; he is the principle and seat of authority; and he is the custodian and director of the power which an organized people possesses.

Under the direction of the leader, a people must be structured in the way best suited to express its organic life. This leads to the theory of cultural totalitarianism, which involves the organization of all aspects of social life for the purposes of the state. No cultural activity—education, economics, art, even religion—has a private life of its own: all such activities must rather be mobilized to serve and give expression to national destiny. The German word, *Gleichschaltung*, "all-on-the-same-circuit," captures vividly the meaning of this totalitarian, corporate vision.

Two further implications, one economic, the other militaristic, have been drawn by fascist thinkers. Since a people or nation is a mystical, organic whole, its economic activities must be not only strong but independent. They are, of course, under the complete supervision of the state and serve the ends of the state; but they must also be self-sufficient and unallied with the economic activities of other peoples. Autarky is thus the economic principle the fascist state must acknowledge.[3] The second implication is militarism. A

---

[2] Although Hitler's version of fascism may be read as claiming that the *Volk* and race—neither, to be sure, equivalent to society—is the basic social reality.

[3] A philosophic source of this idea is J. G. Fichte's "The Closed Commercial State" (1800), the Introduction to which is translated in A. Fried and R. Sanders, eds., *Socialist Thought: A Documentary History*, Garden City, 1964.

people, a nation, fascists argue, is not only born in conflict, but struggle, work, the mastery of conflict, strengthen a people's will and promote fascist virtues. Hence fascism rejects pacificism as a general doctrine, and finds war to be a necessary and proper expression of the state. Mussolini coupled his militarism with a dream of empire, as Hitler sought to conquer the "living space" necessary for the Third Reich.

The fascist position on the other problems examined in the text, namely law, obligation, and justice, may now be given. Since the State is understood as the foundation of all rights and values, the legal position of the individual is always related to the state and is conditioned by the virtue of duty. The legal system is developed, not for the sake of the individual but for the purposes of the state, which is filled with life, power, and purpose as suitable fields of action are secured for the individual. Legal positions with their accompanying rights and obligations thus represent the organic fixation of individuals in the living order. As these relations are organic, no distinct problem of political obligation really arises. Individuals can have no other obligation except that of obedience to the state as the support and fulfillment of their lives. Finally, since the state is the origin of all values, there can be no ideal of justice, or claim for justice, outside the state itself.

At the beginning of this Appendix, mention was made of the eclectic character of fascist theory. Some of its sources can be briefly identified, though caution must be used relative to the accuracy of fascist interpretations and adaptations of them. Organic theories of society were developed by philosophers like Plato, Fichte, Hegel, and some of the medieval realists. Political absolutism found philosophic expression in Machiavelli, Hobbes, and some older supporters of monarchy. Irrationalism, with a concomitant emphasis on action, the life of feeling, and the will to power, may be read into the philosophy of many romantics and of Nietzsche, who was especially admired by Hitler. Mussolini also referred occasionally to the pragmatism of fascism, as well as to Thomas Carlyle's theory of the hero—a theory some also find in Hegel. The embrace of fascism with violence has connections with the views on violence developed by Georges Sorel.[4]

[4] See his *Reflections on Violence* (1905–1906), which is widely anthologized.

The history of the major fascist experiments in Italy and Germany is a short one, lasting only from the 1920's to the end of World War II in 1945. Most of the basic fascist literature dates from this period as well, although commentaries and criticisms of the theory continue to be produced to the present day.

Bibliographical Essay

A number of studies present materials on fascism, including the Library of Congress publication, *Fascism in Action*, U. S. Government Printing Office, 1947; Albert R. Chandler, *The Clash of Political Ideals*, New York, 1949, 1957; and Carl Cohen, *Communism, Fascism, and Democracy*, New York, 1962. Writers usually anthologized include Alfredo Rocco (1875–1935), fascist minister of justice; Giovanni Gentile (1875–1944), Italian philosopher; Mario Palmieri, who published *The Philosophy of Fascism* in Chicago in 1936; Alfred Rosenberg (1893–1946), whose *The Myth of the Twentieth Century* (1930) was a major apology for German racism; and such leaders of the Nazi party as Göring and Goebbels. Both Mussolini and Hitler produced their own statements of fascism, Mussolini in an article in *Enciclopedia Italiani* and in *The Doctrine of Fascism*, Florence, 1936, and Hitler in *Mein Kampf* and his collected speeches.

Critical works abound, and only a sample of them can be noted here. Histories of political theory, of which G. H. Sabine, *A History of Political Theory*, New York, 1954, is still one of the best, often contain comparative if not critical surveys. Hannah Arendt's many articles on political theory, as well as her *The Origins of Totalitarianism*, New York, 1951, are insightful; and two older studies remain invaluable: Albert L. Chandler, *Rosenberg's Nazi Myth*, Ithaca, New York, 1945, and Ernst Cassirer, *The Myth of the State*, New Haven, 1946. A more recent study is A. James Gregor, *The Ideology of Fascism*, New York, 1969.

Glossary

Many of the basic words and concepts of social philosophy are defined in the text. For their meanings, number entries in the *Index* should be consulted; this Glossary does not include all of them. However, as is frequently the case in a philosophical work, technical words are occasionally used or mentioned without specific definition. The following Glossary is provided to assist the reader in understanding them. For fuller statements of their meaning, standard dictionaries of philosophy may be consulted.

Absolute, the term used primarily by idealists for the unconditioned, true, and inclusive metaphysical reality.

Absolutism, political form of government in which political power is exercised in unqualified or unlimited ways.

Actual, actuality existing in act or fact; the real. In Aristotle, the condition in which all potentiality is realized.

Alienation the state or condition of being separated or divided from what is appropriate to an individual.

Altruism theory that one's motivation or moral principle should be to have regard for others; opposed to selfishness or egoism.

Analytic jurisprudence position in legal theory holding that the primary task of jurisprudence is the clarification of fundamental legal conceptions and relations.

Analytic proposition a statement or proposition whose truth value can be determined by logical analysis alone; sometimes called a tautology.

Anarchy theory or state of the absence of government; sometimes, more broadly, the nonrecognition of authority in any sphere.

Autarky theory of economic self-sufficiency for a society.

Authority right or power to enforce obedience, to command, or to give an ultimate decision; also, an expert on any question.

Autonomy literally, self-rule or self-government. Principle that one should be a law unto oneself. Frequently opposed to authority.

Being that which truly is; object of study of traditional metaphysics.

Bourgeoisie members of the mercantile or shop-keeping class of a society. In Marx, owners of the means of production and distribution.

Class a division or grouping of members of a society according to status, rank, or function.

Conservatism political position marked by a tendency to preserve and keep relatively intact existing institutions.

Convention among the ancients, principles accepted on the basis of agreement; opposed to natural which identified principles believed rooted in the natures of things.

Custom a habitual or usual practice; in law, a usage which by continuance has acquired the force of law.

Deontological an ethical theory which places moral worth in an inherent principle or value of will, in contrast to ends or purposes achieved.

Determinism doctrine or theory that every event is the necessary consequence of antecedent causal chains.

Dialectic process of thought (sometimes reality as well) in which opposites or contradictions are taken to merge into higher unities which synthesize them.

Egoism theory that one's motivation or moral principle is self-regarding; opposed to altruism.

Emotivism, emotive theory theory that moral statements function as expressions of emotion, not as cognitive appraisals.

Empiricism epistemological theory that the source and criterion of knowledge are to be found in experience.

Equity in jurisprudence, the recourse to general principles of justice to supplement the ordinary law.

Evaluation the act of determining the worth or value of anything.

Exploitation the act of using another for one's own, usually selfish, interests.

Federalism political theory holding that two or more states constitute a political unity while remaining independent in regard to at least some of their internal affairs.

Good generally synonymous with value; a term of commendation relative to states of affairs or persons and their qualities.

Hedonism from the Greek, hedoné, pleasure; used of theories which make pleasure the proper end of human action.

Humanism system of thought or action which is concerned primarily with human needs and interests.

Ideal statement of what ought to be; a definition of a good or value.

Ideology a system of ideas (sometimes taken to be false or at least nonscientific) which guides or determines human actions.

Intellectual virtue a good of, or relative to, the intellect; in Aristotle, a habit of right functioning in knowing.

Jurisprudence the science which treats of human laws and legal systems in general; sometimes, the philosophy of law.

Justification providing warrant for some conclusion by referring to principles believed supportive of that conclusion.

Legal realism school of jurisprudence which seeks to study the law scientifically, with particular reference to sociological data which influence law and legislation.

Liberalism philosophically (in this book), the cluster of political ideas associated with John Locke and those influenced by them; politically, a position favorable to change and reform, generally in the direction of welfare democracy.

Materialism in metaphysics, theory that reality is matter or the material; in economics, theory that the primary and causal social reality is the economic order.

Metaethics literally, before ethics. Philosophical discipline which attempts to reflect on and analyze primary moral experience and judgments.

Moral philosophy generally, synonymous with ethics. Sometimes used to refer to philosophic activities which attempt to relate ethics to a broader philosophic view.

Moral virtue a good of, or relative to, human action; in Aristotle, a habit of right functioning of desire.

Nihilism from the Latin *nihil*; view that no value, meaning, goal or purpose is available to human life.

Norm, normative having to do with what ought to be in contrast to what is.

Obligation what is laid upon one relative to what ought to be done; a duty.

Oligarchy form of government in which power is confined to a few.

Ontology subdivision or branch of metaphysics which seeks to investigate the principles of being as such.

Organic, organicism generally used in social philosophy to refer to theories which hold that society is a whole of dependent, interrelated individuals, or that the whole is prior to the part.

Paternalism principle that government should act toward its citizens in ways to secure their good for them, even—in the strong sense of the word—against their explicit wishes if necessary.

Political obligation that which is laid upon one relative to what ought to be done, with particular reference to the social and political order.

Politics the science or art of governing the affairs of a society, with reference to the perceived interests of citizens and the form and organization of the state.

Potency, potentiality not yet existent or real; capable of being actualized, though not yet in that state of being.

Power possession of control or command over others; legal ability or authority to act.

Proletariat the class of wage-earners who have no reserve or capital; sometimes, all wage-earners.

Proposition in logic, the meaning of a declarative sentence; a unit of discourse which can be true or false.

Rationalism epistemological theory that the source and criterion of knowledge are reason.

Secularism a position which attempts to formulate or to conclude with assertions independently of all religious convictions and frameworks.

Self-realization in ethical theory, the fulfillment of the possibilities of development of the self; normatively, that such fulfillment is the basic ethical imperative.

Skepticism doubt, sometimes denial, of the possibility of human knowledge or its attainment.

Social engineering phrase used for the view that governmental power and policy should be mobilized to "engineer" the achievement of the general welfare.

Synthetic proposition: a proposition whose truth value cannot be determined by analysis alone and which must therefore be referred to experience.

Teleological ethical theory an ethical theory which places moral worth in the ends or consequences of human action, not in some inherent principle of will.

Teleology literally, study of ends or purposes; also, theories which identify or rest on purpose as a basic principle.

Valuation the actual experience of value, in contrast to acts of evaluation or appraisal.

Value generally synonymous with good; that which is desired, approved, sought after, the actual experience of prizing or enjoying.

Virtue a moral good relative to personal conduct; in Greek thought, the habit of right functioning.

Wisdom generally, a grasp of the basic principles or truths of some domain of human experience and a knowledge of their appropriate application in that domain.

Index